Alexander Michie

Missionaries in China

Alexander Michie

Missionaries in China

ISBN/EAN: 9783743305533

Manufactured in Europe, USA, Canada, Australia, Japa

Cover: Foto ©Andreas Hilbeck / pixelio.de

Manufactured and distributed by brebook publishing software (www.brebook.com)

Alexander Michie

Missionaries in China

MISSIONARIES

IN

CHINA.

BY

ALEXANDER MICHIE

(TIENTSIN).

LONDON: EDWARD STANFORD,
26 & 27, COCKSPUR STREET, CHARING CROSS, S.W.
1891.

INTRODUCTION.

THE friends of the author of the following essay, to whose care it has been intrusted for publication, consider that a few introductory remarks regarding the events which have been the immediate cause of its production may be of use to English readers, whose information regarding the recent riots in China must necessarily be slight and vague. Knowledge of foreign countries, even those with which we have constant communication and important interests, is not so general as it ought to be, and comparatively few persons in England comprehend how closely this country is touched by any occurrence that might lead to estrangement or rupture between England and China.

The cotton weavers of England clothe multitudes of Chinese, whilst in return the Chinese cultivator and merchant find profitable customers amongst ourselves. So it comes that working populations on opposite sides of the globe, who know almost nothing of each other, are constantly contributing to their mutual sustenance and comfort. On the other hand, a large number of the best of our people, filled with the unselfish desire of giving the blessings of Christianity to the Chinese, support a staff of missionaries, who, whatever opinion may be held regarding their methods, are undoubtedly, as a class, actuated by high and unselfish motives. Whatever, therefore, tends to produce estrangement between the Chinese and the English tends to diminish the wealth and material comforts of both countries, and tends to retard, if not to destroy, the spread in China of the form of religion which has been associated with the highest development of morality, self-sacrificing sentiment, and spiritual refinement, which the world has yet seen.

Those who are best acquainted with the relations of Europeans to the Chinese are thus best able to realise the gravity of the news which has come from China intermittingly during the last few months. Even people who know nothing of these relations were shocked to read of brutal attacks of Chinese mobs on unoffending men and women; but those who can appreciate what is under the surface must realise not only that acts of gross cruelty have been perpetrated, but that the evidence goes only too strongly to indicate that as regards a better understanding of foreigners by the Chinese, the work of a generation, with all its sacrifices, appears to have been thrown away. Great as the disappointment must be to those who wish best to the Chinese people, the loss to the Chinese themselves is more serious, for it is clear that the longer the estrangement lasts between the civilised world and the Chinese, the longer must the progress of that patient and laborious people remain at the mercy of a bureaucracy, whose direct personal interests are furthered by the exclusion of foreign thought and foreign inventions.

Unfortunately, the attacks on Christians and Christian missions cannot be considered as exceptional or isolated. After the cruel massacre at Tientsin, which occurred in 1870, little was heard for a time of attacks on mission establishments. The reparation that was then exacted, although considered by some to have been insufficient, was evidently enough to overawe for a time the instigators of these anti-foreign riots; but the feeling that led to them had not disappeared. A few years ago, at Chung King, in the far west of China, the French Catholic mission houses were destroyed, and Chinese Christians killed, there being no motive for the outrages except the anti-Christian sentiment of the Chinese gentry.

To pass over minor outrages, we come to the present year—1891, when we find a Roman Catholic cathedral burnt and the English consulate wrecked at Wuhu; and a Custom House officer and a missionary killed, and the mission buildings destroyed at Wusueh in riots instigated by fanatics. The virulence of this anti-Christian feeling is shown by the fact that at Kiang Yin, on the Yangtze, the mob disinterred the bodies of missionaries who had been buried for two hundred years. At Wooseih, on the Grand Canal near Soochow, a missionary establishment was burnt down. At Ichang, three hundred miles above Hankow, the Roman Catholic and Protestant establishments were destroyed, whilst points so distant as Foochow in the South and Kirin, in Manchuria, have shown evidences of the anti-Christian conspiracy. We read of attempts to excite the populace at Foochow by virulent placards; and at Kirin, Dr. Greig, an able and devoted medical missionary, for whom grateful Chinese patients had erected a dispensary, was treacherously attacked, most cruelly treated, and seriously injured; whilst, according to a recent telegram, a Belgian priest and several Christians have been put to death in Eastern Mongolia.

Sad as it is to read of these gross outrages on unoffending people, the future appears still more ominous when we consider the means by which the *literati* and gentry lashed the passions of the poor and ignorant, but pacific, populace into action. For many long months, illustrated sheets, whose contents are of a nature to defy description, were gratuitously given away by pawnbrokers (who in China have always some official rank, and occupy a semi-official position), and were placarded on walls, under the eyes of the mandarins who could have suppressed them in a day. Gross caricatures of the figures which in Christendom are most reverenced, and association of the most sacred

Christian themes with the vilest obscenities, persistently brought to the notice of—sad to say—persons of both sexes and all ages, must have injured, for a long time to come, the capacity for reverencing the Christian faith; whilst the filthy anti-Christian songs which the children have been taught to sing in the streets, and the foul pictures associated with missionaries which have been brought freely before them, is a proof of how lamentably these ignorant people are in want of the better and higher ideal at which all Christian communities aim. This association of Christianity with ribaldry and foulness is one of the least hopeful facts connected with the outrages.

There is no doubt that under the pressure of the Powers whose subjects have been outraged (England being most directly concerned) some of the guilty, and certainly some of the mob, will be severely punished. Possibly, if the pressure is sufficiently firm, some of the mandarins who allowed the riots to take place may be more or less disgraced; and of course the proffered money compensation will be accepted. Foreign Governments may, indeed, take so comprehensive a view of the situation as to insist on satisfaction of such a nature that the mandarins may not allow riots of this kind to occur again for a generation. But the suppression and prevention of outward disturbances cannot change the current of men's thoughts; the hatred of Christianity will remain, and the difficulty of converting the Chinese to Christianity is enormously increased. That Christian missionaries in China and medical missionaries, now more handicapped than ever, will continue to devote themselves to the Chinese, however unwilling these are to receive them, may be taken for granted; but the problem of how best to live down and overcome the prejudice which has been created, must give occasion for much thought to reflective minds. One of the tasks, and not the least difficult, to which their energies must be applied, is to preach and extend

Christianity in such a way as to render misrepresentation difficult, and the credence of slanderous lies impossible.

It is largely as a contribution to the solution of this problem that the writer of the following pages appears to have composed his essay. He possesses eminent qualifications for the task, having resided many years in various parts of China, and having been in intimate association with all classes of Chinese and foreigners who are found in that country. He writes with the advantage of a full and ripe experience. Few who read what he has written will doubt that he has chosen the right time to open for discussion a subject which, in the nature and magnitude of its interests, is of an importance which it is impossible to over-rate.

LONDON, *November* 1891.

CONTENTS.

	PAGE
INTRODUCTION	v
I.—POLITICAL	5
II.—RELIGIOUS	29
III.—MODUS VIVENDI	71

APPENDICES.

I.—Article in 'Les Missions Catholiques,' by Rev. L. E. Louvet	94
II.—Memorial on the recent Outrages on the Yangtze	97
III.—How an Anti-Christian Riot is Organised	101
IV.—Abstract of Mission Statistics	106

MISSIONARIES IN CHINA.

For a full exposition of that branch of the great Missionary question which particularly affects China, the data either do not exist, or are not accessible, and if they were, the task of collating them would be an exceedingly laborious one, and could only be achieved by some person possessing special qualifications. The march of events, however, does not wait for exhaustive treatises, and on an obscure subject a little light is better than none at all. Were it only to provoke comment, and contradiction even, such a fugitive essay as the present may serve a useful purpose, for the subject is really one of the most important of the day. Not missionaries alone, nor statesmen, are interested in the propagation of Christianity; men of every shade of opinion and with the most diverse sympathies cannot help recognising, whether they approve it or not, the dynamic force of a religion which splits up nations as frost does the solid rock. As a potent factor, for good or ill, in the re-birth of the great Asiatic peoples, the missionary movement commands the attention of every man and woman who, by political, commercial, or merely humane incentives, is drawn into cogitations on the possible destiny of these ancient races.

From the nature of the case the information on the subject is almost entirely in the hands of the Missionaries themselves. The evidence of the natives, which would be invaluable, is not obtainable, for when they do speak out they do not speak frankly. The all important consideration, therefore, how the overtures of the missionaries are received by those to whom they are addressed, can scarcely be got at by direct means, but only by inference—often of a very indirect character. Busy as they may be, the working missionaries do spare a little of their time for investigations into their ways and means of progress; and their periodical Conferences, such as those held in Shanghai in 1877 and in 1890, the latter attended by upwards of 400 missionaries, half of them being women, bring together from all parts of the Chinese empire the fruits of wide experience; and they afford opportunities for a healthy interchange of opinions between men who have been labouring in many different fields. It is, however, hardly to be expected that the deliberations of the working missionaries should extend to matters outside of a well defined province. Their self searchings, earnest enough so far as they go, are mostly narrowed down to matters where the world at large either cannot or does not care to follow them. Their deliberations, in fact, usually stop at the point where the thoughtful public would like them to begin; matters which to the ordinary man seem essential being either avoided altogether, or voted peremptorily out of the discussion. Their aims they consider settled beyond controversy, their methods they assume to be consecrated by the example and precept of their Founder; and, with these axiomatic truths as a basis, they are in the habit of summing up their success by the arithmetical formula by which sportsmen count their game; so many missionaries in the field, so many baptisms. Not that they disregard the quality of either their evangelists or converts. Very far from it; they apply the most rigid tests to both; only the matter once settled, it is settled, and the numerical sign is then all that is needed to express the value of their work. It is, however, just those questions which evangelists and theologians of all colours insist on treating as closed that the rest of mankind are most interested in keeping open; and in that lies the *crux* of the controversy which for an indefinite

* ".... The lack of spiritual discernment on the part of the great bulk of his converts. ... The truths that are lodged in their intellects, and which they accept as unquestionable verities, do not appear to move them deeply. Their spiritual nature is not intensely quickened and greatly expanded by 'the things of the Spirit of God,' neither are their moral activities powerfully energised by them. They lack that divinely-illumined, soul-transforming apprehension of spiritual truth," &c.—Rev. Griffith John, Shanghai Conference, 1877.

time to come must divide the smaller from the larger world of thought.

Those who are most honestly opposed to unrestricted propagandism among anciently civilised races are well aware that it cannot be stopped so long as the fervour of religious passion which is behind the movement shows no signs of abatement. They, however, watch the movement, not without anxiety. For even if in Western Christendom, in its modern condition of comparative equilibrium, religion still constitutes one of the chief difficulties of civil government, to what uncertainties must not the hot aggression of a strange religion give rise among the teeming populations of the East! The remote or collateral effects of their action disturb the repose, or, to do them more justice, interrupt the labours, of the working missionaries but little; which is reason the more why the public should seek to gain a clearer comprehension of the question, and why the societies should give earnest heed to their heavy responsibility in equipping and commissioning so formidable an army and sending it into fields so far from their observation. In the following pages nothing more than partial glimpses, more suggestive than satisfying, are attempted; and the aim of the writer will be fully attained if the thoughtful reader is put upon further enquiry into a pregnant subject.

I. POLITICAL.

Under the political aspect of the question may be conveniently included the whole external relations of mission work in China to governments, people, and institutions. A few prominent features which challenge the attention of the most hasty observer are, however, all that need trouble us at present.

In the first place, the recognition of missionaries was forced on China by the treaties made with foreign powers whom China could not resist, and recent occurrences show that those powers from time to time interfere, with effect, for their protection. In what light the missionaries regard such interference is a question of secondary importance. Some we know to be professedly opposed to "the arm of flesh" being stretched out in their behalf; but when trouble comes upon them there is a loud and pretty unanimous outcry among missionaries for the avenging sword, and considerable impatience is evinced when it is slow in appearing.

Secondly: Toleration of Christian missionaries, extorted by force from China, placed Christians on a different platform from the other foreign religions, Mohammedanism and Buddhism, to which

China of its own motion extended complete toleration. Christianity is therefore inseparably associated with the humiliation of the empire, a calamity which is yet fresh in the memory of the living generation.

Thirdly: the sole ground on which toleration was claimed for Christianity was that it taught men to be virtuous. Only in the German treaty, made subsequently to the others, was this qualification omitted. The Chinese, however, see that if Christianity teaches virtue it also does many other things not specified in their treaties; and the people, circumstanced as they are—innately suspicious and fearful of change—have some difficulty in recognising in the actual Christianity of real life the innocent disguise which theoretical Christianity was made to wear when presented to them at the point of the bayonet.

Fourthly: From whatever cause or combination of causes, missionaries of every creed—and they are varied enough—have aroused the detestation of the people of China of all classes.

This last is a fact of supreme importance. The missionaries—and small blame to them—would fain explain it away by alleging that the hostility evinced against them comes all from the literate and official class, and that popular risings are instigated by that class alone, or, as in the great rising of 1891, by secret societies organised in alliance with them. It has long been a convenient fiction whereby foreigners who are not missionaries console themselves for the open-mouthed hatred of the educated and ruling classes that the mass of the people are, if not actively friendly, at least passively so. It would, however, be a daring discrimination for foreigners and strangers to make in any country, that of drawing a line of demarcation between the feelings of the articulate and of the inarticulate sections of the people. Even where "hereditary bondsmen" have for their spokesmen only men belonging virtually to an aristocratic order, it would not be safe for outsiders to assume any wide disparity of sentiment—as regards external matters. And, considering the essentially democratic basis of Chinese polity, and how the educated class is recruited from the *bourgeoisie*, and even from the peasantry, no one would come to the conclusion *a priori* that the learned would be likely to nourish feelings which were essentially unpopular. Appearances, no doubt, often favour the fond conceit of foreigners that the people are with them. In moving about the country foreigners are seldom molested; they sometimes even find sociable travelling companions among the natives; and in more or less temporary residences in the interior, individuals, whether from curiosity or good feeling, or both, make themselves agreeable to strangers. Yet the universal tendency for mobs to gather round stray foreigners, the rough way they press upon travellers even into the rooms of their inn, the volleys of foul epithets, and even of clods and stones always ready to descend on the slightest suggestion, seem to betray a substratum of ill-feeling covered by a very thin crust of civility. Children of three years in country villages lisping opprobrious names the first time they see a foreigner tell a tale which can hardly be misunderstood as to the real chronic feelings of the populace. To the credit of the missionaries, it must be said that wherever they settle they gain the affections of many of the natives. It is admitted, however, that those natives who conciliate the missionaries lose caste among their own neighbours, a fact which indicates with sufficient clearness the direction of the main current of feeling. In short, the theory of the friendliness of the Chinese people as distinguished from the learned classes cannot bear the stress of the evidence against it.

It is admitted that the enmity of the *literati* only finds its ultimate concrete expression in risings of the populace. But the people are always and everywhere ready to rise at a moment's notice. Could they possibly be worked upon in this manner by the artificial infusion from without of feelings which they did not share? In isolated cases such a thing might happen, but the indefinite repetition of it would be impossible, for, after all, the Chinaman is constitutionally passive; inertia, indeed, is his chief characteristic; and overt aggressive action requires the stimulus of overmastering feelings.

It must, therefore, we fear, be conceded that hatred of missionaries is practically universal throughout China, since there is no part of the country where mobs cannot be set upon them with the same certainty as a pack of hounds is put on the trail of a fox. The converts and adherents form around individual mission stations a thin margin of neutral and even friendly sentiment, but "China's Millions" are as a body dead against them, and their native followers are the first object of attack when the mobs rise. What is more, the hostile feeling is obviously increasing in intensity, and spreading with the spread of the missionaries themselves.

This, then, is the dominant fact in the situation, which demands strict investigation at the hands of all missionary bodies and of all governments who by force of arms maintain them. For if the missionaries misunderstand the attitude of the Chinese nation, they may be heaping up obstacles to the entrance of Christianity, not now only, but for all future time; and if foreign governments misunderstand it they may be betrayed into a course of action which will feed the fires of hate, to the lasting damage of both Chinese and foreigners.

Were it possible to get down to the fundamental cause of the Chinese national hostility to foreign missions, the achievement would be worthy of infinite labour. Let us hope the attempt will one day be seriously made by some competent hand. On the mere surface of things, however, are several concurrent causes the combination of which seems sufficient to account, provisionally, for the phenomenon. The missionaries, speaking of them generally, are not unnaturally disposed to evade the enquiry, and to take shelter in certain biblical platitudes (platitudes as so used) which represent the hatred of the world as the natural inheritance of the true Church. It is always interesting, and often highly instructive, to discover in ancient writings pictures of modern events, but the habit of resorting to the Scriptures, as to a ready-made clothes shop, for descriptions and explanations of transactions which take place under our own eyes must tend to mental degeneration and to the suppression of the manly habit of candid open-eyed observation. When the Chinese cite their own classics in support of their attitude towards Christianity the missionaries justly scoff at the fallacy. Equally adverse to sound conclusions is the anti-scientific temper which is induced in the missionaries by the vicious practice of shunning common terms for describing common things, and of falling back on imperfectly understood phrases which have been stereotyped for thousands of years.

Against the easy-going assumption of the missionaries that when they are hated it is their

Master who is hated, there stands the broad historical fact, in China, of toleration and patronage extended to the two great foreign religions, Mohammedanism and Buddhism. Nor can this be explained away by the simple device of referring these religions to diabolic invention. So far as religion pure and simple is concerned the Chinese bear the palm among all the nations of the earth for toleration; and the presumption is therefore irresistibly strong that it is never the religious but some other element in the missionary propaganda that rouses the passions of the Chinese. Instead of exciting them to wrath, indeed, the standing wonder is that Christianity, being what it is, and the condition of the average Chinese being what it is, the common people do not hear it gladly, for the promise of bliss to those doomed to the dismal life of the Chinese masses, and who are ready to believe anything, must, one would think, be like a sunbeam lighting the recesses of a prison. This is the strange thing that calls for explanation, not by cut-and-dried dicta from the old Scriptures, but by candid examination of the facts of the case, such as will satisfy any well-balanced mind. While waiting for such explanation the missionaries must stand provisionally responsible for either so misunderstanding their message, or so mismanaging the delivery of it, as to render it virtually of no effect over the larger portion of their field of operations.

The preliminary obstacle to the reception not

only of missionaries, but of foreigners and foreign ideas of every kind, is that most intractable sentiment of race hatred which is common to all mankind. This has to be confronted like a natural phenomenon as a constant factor in all international problems; and of all peoples on the face of the earth the English-speaking races have the least reason to be surprised at finding it among the Chinese. The contemptuous way the English commonalty have of speaking of "nasty dirty furriners" is evidence enough of the strength of the race antipathy of the English; and if more specific testimony were wanting it would be furnished from the works of all modern travellers. Sir Charles Dilke, in his "Problems of Greater Britain" (Vol. I., p. 357), says: "The dislike of the Australians for the Chinese is so strong and so general that it is like the dislike of terriers for rats. . . . Nothing will so rapidly bring together an Australian crowd as the rumour that Chinamen or rabbits are likely to be landed from a ship, and one class of intruder is about as popular as the other." Substituting "foreign missionaries" for "Chinamen" and for "Australian" "Chinese," the description would fairly describe the state of feeling in China, only with the proviso that the Chinese keep their feelings under better control than Australians, Californians, or any other branch of the white Christian family.

And the feeling in China is unhappily aggravated by those very considerations of benefits conferred which, with the self-complacency almost peculiar to the Anglo-Saxon forms of Christianity, the missionary bodies expect to alleviate it. China indeed cherishes a traditional hospitality to strangers from the Four Seas, and is in this respect more liberal than most other states. But then such strangers must come as guests and suitors, looking up to the central nation as their protector. To such the imperial bounty will ever be extended, as to shipwrecked Loochooans or other derelict persons. It is in no such guise that the Western foreigners present themselves in China. They are successful rebels against the Middle State, her guests only by the right of the stronger. We say we have many good qualities, also good gifts to bestow on China, including the knowledge of things in Heaven and earth of which the Chinese, in their classical pride, are ignorant. Does such a pretension as that gain us favour in their eyes? Ought it to do so? According to the invariable working of the human mind the attainments of which we boast, and the superfine moralities which we profess with not a little braying of trumpet, are the things most calculated to excite the hatred, not unmixed with fear, of the people on whom we have so brusquely intruded. And as a matter of fact, all the State papers and other publications of Chinese, when not dictated by foreigners, under threats, or written to serve a special need, are as the unloading of stores of burning hatred from the breasts of their authors.

Such being the normal attitude of Chinese officials and people towards foreigners in general and missionaries in particular, the next thing to consider is what inducements have been or can be held out, or what means employed to break down or reduce this great wall of opposition either by individuals or by the different sections of foreigners. Obviously the mercantile classes have the best of this, as the benefits they confer on the Chinese people are patent and need no recondite explanation. Their influence, however, does not penetrate below the surface of things, and is not felt beyond their own immediate surroundings; it is barren and incapable of propagation.

The missionaries are so much less favourably situated than the merchants in that they have no *raison d'être* intelligible to the Chinese, and consequently their presence everywhere breeds mystery. Even in isolated cases where they meet with personal kindness they are nevertheless objects of suspicion. A lady of the China Inland Mission relates in *China's Millions* for June, 1891, how her party was graciously received by the wife of a mandarin in one of their peregrinations in the province of Sechuan. The mandarin himself was in an adjoining room, whence he plied the missionary ladies with questions, through his wife and another native woman. " He wanted, of course, to know why we had come? Were we going to trade? Had we brought anything to sell? Who had sent us? Were we going to rent a house? How long were we going to stay? Had our Queen sent us to China?" In her lively gossipping manner Miss Williams here lets in a strong side-light on the missionary position. The catechism of her mandarin probably epitomises the best thoughts of the Chinese regarding missionaries.

It is a fact to the credit of the missionaries that in many localities—indeed, more or less at every place where they have settled—they have established confidence and "rubbed down prejudice," as an old missionary summarised his own work of twenty years in one city. And often, by means of cures effected on wives of officials or other services rendered, they gain a footing in the Yamêns. In this way relations of real friendship are extending in many provinces. These, however, are, after all, isolated cases which do not sensibly diminish the mass of opposition. The good influence of the missionaries is spreading—such, at least is the natural inference from their published reports; but the important question is whether the adverse influences are not increasing in a more rapid ratio. Is the water in the ship's hold gaining on the pumps? Every success, we may take for granted, provokes fresh opposition, and the best opinion seems to lean in the direction of the opposing wave rising and threatening to overwhelm the whole propaganda.

So composite is the missionary body that to arrive at concrete truth in regard to it each of its many members would have to be examined separately—an impossible task. As, however, it is certain that the Chinese officials and people take no account of the varieties of missionary, the different sections of the force which dislike each other's ways (only in a less degree than the Chinese themselves do) being all classed in the lump, it will be sufficient also for our present purpose to take them *en bloc*. The reputation of each section reacts on the whole body.

One of the chief grounds of opposition to Christianity, one which grows naturally out of what has been above advanced, is that the Catholic Church has, ever since the Treaties of 1858–60, and even since the French Treaty of 1844, been associated with the aggressive policy of France; a power which has been suspected of cherishing designs against China, and which has employed the missionaries as political and even military spies. The conviction that this causes frequent outbreaks against missions is growing among the Catholic missionaries, who remark (see Appendix I.) that they have suffered much more at the hands of the Chinese since France openly took them under her protection for her own purposes than when they enjoyed no protection from any foreign power.

And even French missionaries are coming to think that they would be better off, and safer, were they to be openly divorced from the military power of France and every other country. All these, however, are considerations which would weigh mainly with the educated classes in China, who are able to keep the run of contemporary history. But the Chinese populace is probably as unable to grasp, as it would be unlikely to spontaneously act upon, the mere political objections to propagandism. If even, therefore, the attitude of the *literati* were rendered fully intelligible by such wide views of the situation, the strong anti-missionary sentiment of the people would still remain to be accounted for. The two forces combined, the guiding spirit of the lettered and the obedient muscles of the unlettered class, are as necessary to the production of outrage as the dual parentage of vertebrates. Without the stimulus of pamphlets scattered broadcast, of placards and harangues to prompt and direct the movement, and without unanimity of feeling in the mass to be moved, there would be no mob violence against missionaries of a general and far-spread character.

The *modus operandi* has come to be pretty well understood. Certain able pens, some of whom are known to belong to the governing classes, are engaged compiling the most atrocious indictments against the missionaries in general, in which they not only travesty and grossly caricature the doctrines and practices of Christianity, but charge the missionaries of both sexes with crimes which it requires a Chinese imagination to conceive. Admittedly able as literary essays, these lampoons are laden with matters which Zola himself would blush to translate into any European language. It may fairly be said that these publications, which are sold at the Government bookshops in every city, reveal the unspeakable foulness of the Chinese mind, while they fail to smirch the garments of the objects of their attack. But that is not, unfortunately, the whole question. Sad as it is to think so, the mass of the people believe all the charges circulated against the missionaries. Were it not so, the pamphleteers are too clever to go on publishing them, for they know their audience well. The authors may not in all cases absolutely believe their own words, though the human mind possesses such an amazing faculty for believing what it wishes that it is possible these literary assailants of foreign missionaries are as sincere as was St. Paul when he deemed the Christians of his day worthy of death by stoning. There is, in fact, abundant evidence that the Chinese officials do believe all these charges. No charges of mere abstract immorality, however, would ever incite any Eastern mob to the fever pitch of virtuous violence; and the attacks of the *literati* would be as harmless as summer lightning were they not barbed by accusations of another kind which directly touch the life of the people at large.

The missionaries are held up to popular odium as kidnappers of children. The crime is so common among the Chinese that the fear of it keeps the villagers in a chronic state of alarm. Hence the allegations against missionaries, already objects of suspicion and aversion, are accepted with eager credulity, needing no proof. The missionaries, it may be said, are fully aware of all this.

It would serve no good purpose here to follow in detail the various medical uses to which foreigners are believed to put stolen children, and the various organs and secretions of the body. They are well known to all those who interest themselves in China missions. No race has a higher reverence for the human form, as such, than the Chinese. All defects and deformities are held in horror by them, and they will rather die than part with a limb. In the case of early mutilations for special purposes the parts are religiously preserved to be eventually buried with the body to which they belonged, so that in the spirit world no blemish may appear. The alleged mutilations by foreigners, therefore, enormously heighten the gravamen of the charges of kidnapping. The belief that the foreign missionaries are habitually guilty of such practices is universal among the Chinese people, and is honestly entertained; even the learned are not free from the same belief.

Against such accusations it is obviously useless for missionaries to protest innocence; the Oriental mind is impervious to demonstration, which is of course the unmanageable feature in the case. Let no one make the mistake of pooh-poohing these extravagances, but remember rather in corroboration the object-lesson which was given in India thirty-five years ago. Convictions were then held by the people of Hindostan as groundless as those now held by the people of China, and official persons first pooh-poohed and then attempted to stifle them. In vain, however, did Government officers expostulate; the designing men who were inciting the popular mind were credited, because the belief on which they were working was deep lodged in the hearts of the people, and the result was one of the great tragedies of history. Let not, therefore, the inherent absurdity or incredible grossness of the Chinese charges against missionaries blind anyone to the plain fact that the Chinese sincerely believe them all. Neither imperial edicts, provincial proclamations, charges of dragoons, nor the headsman's axe, are able to eradicate the conviction. Provincial officials have been sometimes blamed by foreigners for treating the popular outcry seriously, and making enquiries instead of at once stamping out the whole clamour as a childish absurdity. The simple truth in such cases is, the officials in question do implicitly believe every word, a fact of which there have been many proofs in their past intercourse with foreigners.

Before going on to other matters it may be as well to glance at the possible share which the missionaries themselves may have innocently had in furnishing pretexts for such charges. Their hospitals alone, where they treat patients free and supply medicines, while they are a great boon to the poor and sick, and are so highly appreciated as to be always crowded with patients, furnish a handle to the enemies of the missionaries to revile them. The orphanages and schools of the Catholic missions are no less objects of suspicion. Miserable and moribund infants are imprudently taken into these establishments. The mortality is necessarily large, and whether the burial be intra- or extra-mural it often attracts dangerous notice from disaffected people, and in times of excitement furnishes fuel to the fire. Indiscretions in connection with hospitals may at any time have serious consequences. One of the worst outbreaks ever recorded, that which occurred to the China Inland Mission at Yangchow in 1868, is said to have been started by the scientific zeal, carelessly guarded, of a doctor, in putting a human fœtus into a bottle, and leaving it exposed to the view of the Chinese attendants. Such accidents are not the cause of the trouble; that lies deeper; but they may often be the occasion—the match will touch the gunpowder already prepared.

Another distinct series of charges against missionaries is that they bewitch the people, and their houses and ground. When there are deaths in a family or in a village, they are never, or seldom, attributed to natural causes, but always to malign influences of one sort or another. Missionaries form a most convenient scape-goat, and in spite of their free dispensaries, indeed often in conseqence of them, they are suspected of giving witch pills and of compassing evil designs against the people. Where no deliberate evil intention is charged the mere presence of the missionaries is a sinister omen. Their houses in the interior also play a very important part in the general scheme of *diablerie*. It is generally known that the Chinese, high and low, are slaves to a weird kind of earth superstition, which is kept alive by geomancers and other interested parties who are employed in choosing sites for houses, graves, &c. Their scheme for conciliating the good influences of the spirits of earth and air, and averting the bad, is of the most elaborate kind, extending not only to such comparatively reasonable matters as the orientation of houses, gardens, &c., but also to the placing of doors and windows, elevation of roofs, &c., and to the relation of the site to the contours of the surrounding ground, to running or standing water, and innumerable other matters of a like kind. One of the common causes of grievance among themselves refers to the spoiling of the *fêng shui* or good luck of a house or a grave by the erection of new buildings, and the Chinese have their own way of warning off aggressive neighbours as effective as the familiar notice "Ancient Lights" so common in city improvements in London. Even important Government concerns, such as railways, have to bow before these popular deities, and are forced either to make a *détour* or keep clear of a protected neighbourhood altogether, according to the influence and standing of the proprietors of the threatened domain.

But as the missionaries spread themselves out in the interior they naturally require houses, and equally naturally aspire to commanding, æsthetic, and salubrious sites. Hateful as the invader is, however, *per se*, he becomes tenfold more so when he is seen planting himself on every high hill and under every green tree, erecting there beautiful (in his own eyes) but outlandish buildings which bring ill-luck to the whole district. As regards this superstition also there is not a shadow of doubt of the perfect sincerity of the popular conviction. The most learned are not exempt from its influence—rather perhaps they are even greater slaves to the professional geomancer than the poor whose superstitions are less worth cultivating. Long intercourse with foreigners seems not to weaken the real hold of the doctrine, although it may induce concealment, for shame. A case came recently under notice of a thoroughly Anglicised Chinese who had some cases of sickness in his family for which he could not account until he had consulted the oracle. The geomancer pointed out in a foreigner's "compound" not far off a certain temporary structure of mats, which he said dominated the luck of the house. Ashamed to confess his belief in such things, the afflicted man dared not ask the foreigner—a friend of his own, who would willingly have done it—to remove his shed, but prepared instead to abandon his commodious family residence and seek less convenient quarters elsewhere. Eventually the *fêng shui* man allowed him to compromise by closing up his former entrances and getting into the house by a back way. From such an instance as this the strength of the geomantic superstition may be inferred, and also the unavoidable offence which must be constantly, though unintentionally, given by foreign missionaries establishing themselves in the interior. It may be mentioned by way of illustrating the universality of such beliefs that the seer in this instance was not an ordinary fortune-teller, exploiting a rich vein of credulity, but was himself a man of rank and culture, a sort of Chinese Guy Mannering, an amateur in occult science, which is a favourite hobby of the wealthy and learned Chinese.

The right to purchase land and build houses is exercised under a clause in the Franco-Chinese Treaty, of which missionaries of other nationalities claim the benefit under the most-favoured-nation clause of their own respective treaties. When it is discovered that a piece of ground has been sold to a foreign missionary, pressure is usually applied to the seller to make him cancel; the authorities refuse to register the transfer on one pretext or another; but when the local official finally gives way and issues the title deeds, there is peace for a time. The people, however, do not acquiesce, and on some convenient occasion, possibly after some deaths, or in a time of scarcity, or when they have been inflamed by agitators, mobs assemble and burn and pillage the establishment, sometimes maltreating the inmates, and sometimes not. Such are the commonplaces of missionary experiences in China.

What share avoidable aggressions or imprudent procedure on the part of the missionaries themselves may have in these constantly recurring agrarian outrages it is impossible to say. We hear the missionaries' version, but never the other side, and no man is impartial in his own cause. Some divisions of the missionary body have moderate views on the subject and seem to consider that the onus of avoiding disturbance rests on them, that their tenure of property in the interior is of doubtful legality, the French Treaty notwithstanding, and they hold themselves ready to retreat whenever circumstances require it. These are the views on which the Church of England missions under Bishop Scott, with some others, are presumed to act, and though they do not escape all the consequences of disputes with the other missions, they seem to be troubled with very few of their own.

It is impossible to follow up the proceedings of missionaries in the interior, but sometimes an opportunity occurs at the Treaty ports of observing their relations with native officials and people. The question of house building has been brought to an interesting phase recently in a place where both sides of the transaction can be studied. A missionary society some three years ago acquired a small but desirable site on the main street of a populous city, just within the wall, on which they desired to erect a chapel. The funds were partly provided by the general foreign community resident at the port, and partly by the missionary society, and the chapel was erected at the cost of about two thousand dollars. Scarcely was it opened, however, when trouble began to fall upon the family of a rich and benevolent man; sickness and death made their home in his house. Suspicion fell on the new chapel, and an agitation was by-and-by set on foot with a view of negotiating for its removal. The head of the family is in real distress, for not only does he fully believe himself in the malign influence of the high building which overshadows him, but the whole of his womankind, of three generations, torment him with their constant wailing. As the only means of getting rid of the offending building and its occupants was to buy them out, the Chinese gentleman made overtures to the missionary gentleman, to whom he offered as "compensation for disturbance" a sum of money more than seven times what the whole land and building cost, and enough to purchase a larger site and build a handsome chapel elsewhere. The missionary was as hard as adamant in standing on his Treaty rights, and closed the negotiations by demanding the sum of $30,000, or fifteen times the value of his property.

The missionary is no doubt as strictly within his legal rights as Shylock thought he was in his little negotiation with Antonio. But there are cases when even legal rights may properly give way to larger considerations. The position of the Chinese gentleman in this case is peculiar. His charities and good deeds have gained him the love and reverence of the whole population, so that if he held up his finger, as he is often urged to do, the chapel would be demolished in two hours. But he is a man of peace and forbearance. Supposing, however, such a case to arise at a distance from all disinterested foreign witnesses, news of some shocking outrage would then be given to the world, and one crime added to the roll of persecution of the Church in China.

So far only the outward accidents of the missionary position in China have been touched upon, yet even these seem to furnish sufficient *primâ facie* ground for the hostile feelings with which foreign missionaries are everywhere received in the country. When we come to glance at the point of contact between the foreign and native religions, as such, still further grounds of hostility will be disclosed. For when all suspicion as to his motives shall have been removed; when he shall have learned to live on amicable terms with his Chinese neighbours, and they to regard him not as a danger, but as a reasonable friend; when there shall be no more local sources of irritation; when, in short, the missionary shall be treated on his proper merits—what then will be his position towards the Chinese? Will it not still be that of a destroyer of their traditions, their morality, their philosophy—in a word, of that on which they build up their national and individual pride, and of all that now sustains them in an orderly and virtuous life? And is it to be expected that the Chinese will regard such radical destruction —while as yet they do not comprehend what is to be given them in exchange—with the cold gravity of speculative philosophers?

II. RELIGIOUS.

PROBABLY in no part of the world did Christianity obtain an easier entrance than into the empire of China, whether we consider its first appearance there in the sixteenth century, or its latest, under the protection of foreign treaties, in the nineteenth. And nowhere, on the face of the matter, was there so inviting a field, either as regards its vast extent, or the sober character and educational training of the people. Yet the result of missionary effort for three hundred years, arithmetically stated, is a muster roll of but 500,000 Catholics (inclusive of children) and under 50,000 Protestant converts (exclusive of children), the latter of course being the fruit of work during the present century. At what a cost of money this numerical result has been effected it might perhaps be possible to calculate, were it ever worth while to appraise spiritual gain by a financial measure. But the cost in men and women is incalculable. Those who have had no experience of the deadening contact of masses of the poorer Chinese, whose ideas, when they have any, run in opposite directions to ours— whose horizon is limited by their neighbour's rice field, and whose chronology is marked by recurring famines—can scarcely conceive the sacrifice which is made of cultured men and women in consigning them to a long life amid such depressing surroundings. And it lends emphasis to the sacrifice, in common estimation, to consider that in numerous instances the exile has divested himself of wealth and social position as well as other ingredients which the world deems most necessary to the cup of human happiness. The physical discomforts, fatigues, and privations incidental to a missionary career appear to be the least part of what has to be endured in the interior of China, and it is indeed wonderful that so many of the missionaries come through the ordeal with seemingly unimpaired intellectual vitality, and with the moral sense so little blunted.

The reason no doubt is that the cause to which such men and women consecrate their lives is for them the highest goal of human endeavour. To some of them their work is so exigent in its claims as almost to exclude all other thoughts and even ordinary recreation. Nothing short of a high ideal could sustain them through their laborious but apparently fruitless years. Their "mission"—speaking of a large section of them—is the delivery of man from the wrath of God, which is to be accomplished through the words which they speak, and not otherwise. No wonder that the missionaries should stagger under the weight of such responsibility. Those who stand outside the torrid zone of religious zeal may marvel to see a few thousand common mortals voluntarily, indeed eagerly, assuming a co-partnership in the eternal purposes, and some may even stand aghast at their daily urging the Almighty to greater activity in the despatch of His own work. Yet what is to the world at large but the wild-fire of fanaticism is to the parties themselves the one assured reality of human life. This has to be borne in mind in judging missionaries, who are entitled to the common privilege of being gauged by their own standard.

The progress and prospects of Christianity in China are, however, matters which interest a vastly wider circle than that of the missionary bodies. The civilised world is justifiably curious to know how the grand enterprise prospers; it is one of the practical public questions of the day; as the quality of the civilisation which is eventually to cover the earth is the issue which is at stake.

We have seen that the palpable result of Christian missions in China has been to excite virulent opposition throughout the country, counterbalanced by half a million converts. This meagre success, as we have also seen, is to some extent at least due to accidents of the external relations of the propaganda, hindrances to the spread of Christianity which are therefore in their nature removable. Should it appear, however, that underlying all these there are real hindrances, either inherent in the Christian principles themselves or inseparable from the missionaries' manner of presenting them, or, again, due to something peculiar in the circumstances of China, the subject would naturally assume a graver aspect.

Taking the last of these alternatives first: the moral condition of the Chinese people differs greatly from that of every other people to whom Christianity has addressed itself; a circumstance which challenges the studious consideration of those who aspire to influencing them. In the first place, the Chinese are very free from religious fanaticism; since the Tang dynasty at all events, say for the last thousand years, their soil has never been reddened by the blood of martyrs to opinion, nor have desolating religious wars disgraced their annals—unless, indeed, the Taiping rebellion of 1850-64 may be so classed, owing to its leader having parodied Christian theology and drawn his inspiration from the Hebrew Scriptures. The Chinese, though a religious people, in every act of life worshipping the unseen, are probably unique among religionists in that in their daily life they follow the teachings of several religions at once.

Such catholicism of feeling might be attributed to coldness of temperament (though hardly to religious apathy) were there no better explanation within reach. But the true reason which obtrudes itself on our notice seems to be the all-pervading influence of the Chinese philosophy. The grand system of ethics, shaped if not created by the sage Confucius, occupies in China a position unlike that of all other systems. The philosophies of the West, from Pythagoras to Spencer, are abstract and Utopian; that of the Chinese is popular and practical. They interest thinkers; this rules the common life of the masses, and has done so continuously for several thousand years. Confucius has indeed been blamed for providing for all the relations of life so completely as to leave no scope for new thought. But this is probably to make too much of the man, and too little of the people. The sayings of a sage could not leaven the life of a whole race for two milleniums unless he were one of the people, a true representative man. Confucius himself disclaimed the title of originator; he was but a transmitter of the thoughts which were prevalent before his day, and in our modern way of speaking he was the natural product of his age and race. The noteworthy thing is that the wisdom of the Ancients has throughout the whole of their authentic history, and never more than in the present era, been to the Chinese the very life-blood of their morality, personal, domestic, social and political.

In presence of modern discussions as to the

basis of ethics* it is important to remark that the grand moral inheritance of the Chinese is apparently quite independent of specific religious sanction; and it is perhaps this neutral character which renders the Confucian ethics so valuable a solvent of all religious acrimony. With this solid ground-work of life, unassailable by faction, the Chinese can afford to deal calmly with all religions, their own aboriginal cults, Taoism with its temples, priesthood and ritual, as well as the systems imported from abroad. Confucianism is, without doubt, the great moderating force, maintaining an even balance among rival creeds, neutralising exclusive claims, and which would also extend to all foreign religions the same hospitality as it accords to the myths and mysteries of indigenous evolution.

We say "would," for Christianity seems to remain outside this comprehensive scheme of toleration, while foreign religions so like it to the Chinese eye as Buddhism and Mohammedanism are hospitably entertained, living on good terms with each other and with aboriginal superstitions under the *Pax Sinensis*. Why the broad charity of Confucianism should have failed only to embrace the supreme human embodiment of Divine charity is one of those deep questions

---

* "Your honesty is *not* to be based either on religion or policy. Both your religion and policy must be based on *it*."
—Ruskin.

which the *soi-disant* Christian world should set itself diligently to answer. The significance of it spreads over a wider area than is contained within the confines of China.

The acts of the latter-day apostles, could they be well examined, would no doubt throw some light on this question. But only fragments of these are accessible, and the light from them is necessarily refracted through the missionary prism. The Catholic missions being under organised authority as regards both doctrine and practice, some general conception of their attitude towards the Chinese may be arrived at. Personal idiosyncrasies are not wanting even among them, and within the pale of the Church men the most liberal and the most bigoted are to be found. Eccentricities, however, are discouraged, and there is an approximation to uniformity in the work and teaching of the Catholic missionaries. The Protestant missions, on the other hand, though sectionally organised, allow infinite latitude to personal peculiarities in actual practice, while in matters of abstract doctrine the denominations seem to be exacting enough. The missions are so scattered, moreover, as to be practically inaccessible to investigators. It must be understood, therefore, that the general remarks which follow rest on very incomplete data, and are subject to large exceptions.

From the official reports of missionaries, from

their contributions to their own periodicals, from the diaries and personal letters which occasionally obtain the like publicity, and from conversations with individuals belonging to several sections, the general deduction to be drawn is that their attitude towards Chinese ethics, philosophy, and religion is that of war to the knife. In order to build the Christian Church they require the site to be cleared, and before securing friendly consideration for their own schemes they insist on the destruction of what already exists. It is especially necessary to qualify this general statement by reference to the many important exceptions, for there are not a few among the missionaries who entertain sincere respect not only for Confucian philosophy but for the native and foreign religions which flourish in China. And in this connection, the great services which missionaries have rendered to the cause of knowledge can never be forgotten. It is to their labours that we owe what we know of the Chinese language and literature. Missionaries compiled the only dictionaries as yet in common use; a missionary translated the classics into English, laying the whole world under perpetual obligation; missionaries have explained the Chinese religions; and a distinguished English missionary, when entering the Temple of Heaven in Peking, put off his shoes because the place was holy. A missionary has quite recently contributed to descriptive anthropology the first attempt at a systematic analysis of the Chinese character, perhaps the first that has been made of any national character. And, turning towards the Chinese side, the missionaries have the credit of awakening thought in the country, and their great industry in circulating useful and Christian knowledge in vernacular publications of various sorts, though comparatively barren of result in its main purpose, has spread the light of Western civilisation far and wide in the empire.

But although missionaries have written books on the Chinese religions, and have honestly laboured to do them justice, the fact remains that the main body are too busy with their own work to spare any serious thought for such subjects; and those who have studied them necessarily approach them with foregone conclusions which detract from the value of their deductions. At one particular station there are fifteen missionaries of different denominations, not more than two of whom have taken any trouble to acquaint themselves with Buddhism. Yet the business of their lives is to supplant, among other things, that religion!

Indifference to the opinions of others and disrespect for their institutions are somewhat characteristic of the race from which Protestant missionaries mostly come. The English-speaking peoples are everywhere masterful and unaccommodating, representatives of force in its various phases, physical, nervous, and moral. They are often feared, sometimes respected—at a distance. They make good laws, and enforce them, but do not often gain, as they deserve, the love of inferior, or any other races. Constitutionally, they seem to be incompetent for anything but a commanding *rôle*; hence they are scarcely the ideal stuff of which to make missionaries to races which inherit adult civilisations. (With undeveloped races the case is, of course, wholly different.) Through the transparent robes of their humility may generally be traced the imperious spirit, impatient of opposition and delay. Missionaries often try, sincerely enough, to live down to their people; but to wear the clothes of the poor and eat their food may be nearer to formal condescension than to true sympathy. The thing needful, the entering freely into the spirit of the people, is of exceedingly rare attainment. Missionaries talk much, and very naturally, of the good things they offer to the Chinese, and the sacrifices they make for them. But gratitude is not awakened in that way, much less love. Natives instinctively fear foreigners, *et dona ferentes*, and the more the gifts are pressed on their attention the more suspicious they naturally become.

The missionaries act naturally in laying hold of the excrescences of Chinese superstitions and practices, and applying to them their own criteria, thereupon condemning them as base and damnable; in disparaging Confucius and his works; scoffing at the polytheistic Buddhists, and pouring contempt on the monotheistic Mohammedans, with indiscriminating scorn. When they have once attached an "ism" to any of these things, its doom is sealed, and Anathema is the only word that remains to be spoken concerning it. The inconvenient morality of the Chinese, when it cannot otherwise be disposed of, is referred, without more ado, to the Father of Imposture. All this may be natural; but the effect of it is no less natural.

There is, however, and notwithstanding the *a priori* judgment of some missionaries, an irrepressible instinct in man, whereby he is able within certain limits to distinguish between good and evil; and the Chinese are not so devoid of the moral sense* as not to appreciate what is good. When, therefore, they hear things which they revere—and which they know by experience to be excellent and elevating—slighted by men and women in broken and barbarous accents, the latent hostility to foreigners and foreign ideas,

---

* "At the close of one of the services a man followed me into the vestry and addressed me thus:—'I have heard you say that Christ can save a man from his sins. Can he save me?' 'What sins have you?' I asked. 'Every sin you can think of.... I am an opium smoker, gambler, fornicator, and everything that is bad.'"—Rev. G. John, at Shanghai Conference, 1877.

which is a constant quantity in the Chinese mind, is not unlikely to be awakened to inconvenient activity.

What must strike any one on reading a series of missionary records—such for instance as the proceedings of the Conferences held at Shanghai—is the extreme subjectiveness of their utterances, in word and writing, and the corresponding absence of objectiveness. Their thoughts are full of themselves, their doctrines, their organisation, their methods, their efforts, their disappointments, their piety, their charity, their humility and self-effacement; while the condition of the Chinese mind and conscience is passed over with some threadbare commonplaces, as if no account need be taken of that great factor in the problem! The lack of sympathetic imagination which Matthew Arnold charged against his British Philistines seems to be so general among the missionaries that it was left for an ordained Chinaman at the last Conference to implore his foreign brethren to have some consideration for the mental condition of the Chinese. "Remember," he said, "we have forty generations (? centuries) of physical inertia, heathenism, and narrow education behind us," than which no wiser or more apposite sentiment was uttered during the whole proceedings. Deprecating the aggressive method, the same speaker begged his foreign colleagues to avoid in conversation or in writing picking out all the worst phases of Chinese character and passing over in silence what was good.*

A courageous missionary, Mr. F. H. James, presented to the Conference a paper on the Chinese moral sects, for which he solicited the sympathy of his brethren, and even urged that the ways of these Chinese seekers after good should be studied with a view to learning something from them, and at least of meeting them "in a Christ-like spirit." It was characteristic of the Conference that the important subject of that paper failed to elicit a single observation from the assembly, while the whole of the day's sitting at which it was read was occupied with profuse discussions on "the missionary: his qualifications, mode of life," "lay agency," "historical review of missionary methods," "preaching to the heathen," "itineration," and a score or two of similar matters, all interesting enough in themselves, though rather like the smoke of the battle which obscures the object of attack. Nor was this a peculiarity of any one day's proceedings. The whole transactions of the Conference were marked by the same characteristic. Every attempt to induce the brethren to enter into the thoughts and feelings of the natives either fell dead on the audience or

---

* "It is a common saying among them that Buddhism, Taoism, and Confucianism agree in one. Yes, in a bowl of rice with two chopsticks in it. This is *the* aspiration of every class of the people both for the present and the future."—Rev. T. P. Crawford, at Shanghai Conference, in 1877.

was stamped out of discussion by a mass vote; and there seems reason to conclude that this particular phase of Philistinism governs the whole missionary system. What, the missionaries seem to argue, signifies this or that native belief or aspiration or practice, when, whatever they may be, the whole must be swept by our besom? To them Chinamen are but a mass of amorphous pulp to be put into the moulds shaped for them in the Western hemisphere. It was not, however, by neglecting the topography of the enemy's country, or even ignoring the personal qualities of the hostile troops that Von Moltke was successful in his campaigns. A council of war which should confine its deliberations to the state of its own forces while treating the condition of the opposing force as *une quantité négligeable* would soon find its plans frustrated, and the flank of its army turned.*

---

* "We should become thoroughly acquainted with the customs of the people, with their mode of thought, and with their literature, that we may adapt our preaching to their understanding, and illustrate the truth by allusions to familiar things."—Rev. D. Z. Sheffield, at Shanghai Conference, 1877.

"We have learned that though a missionary in time past might have spent his life imagining he was speaking the native language and turning men to God, when he was doing no such thing, *being deceived by the peculiarities of his circumstances and the difficulty of knowing what goes on in a Chinese heart*, home, and community, yet such room for mistake is lessening. We have learned some lessons, and may be encouraged to go on learning, so as to be able to teach."—Rev. J. Sadler, *The Messenger*, 1889.

Supposing that the purely religious element, with its supernatural sanction and unanswerable appeals from the seen to the unseen, were eliminated from this problem, and that an attempt were to be made by ordinary, rational, human means to subvert the civilisation of the Chinese and substitute that of Western Christendom, how would the agents employed in such an enterprise probably proceed? Would they not endeavour to discover some common ground whereon they could meet those whom they sought to change, and, avoiding rather than courting exasperating conflicts with the extremest discrepancies between the Eastern and Western developments, would they not go back, if possible, to their point of original divergence, and then by tracing the causes and the course of the differentiation get behind the present appearances of things, and gain a practical comprehension of what they see, and a sound basis of influence? Would they not, in a word, go to the root of the matter instead of smiting the branches, recognising the necessity of "putting yourself in his place" as a condition of gaining lasting influence over any human soul? Is it the confirmed habit of taking their principles of action too exclusively from the stereotyped verbal dicta of ancient, and often misunderstood, authorities that leads the missionaries to read the motions of the human mind so differently from other men?

It is obvious that the moral systems of the

extreme East and the extreme West have developed in almost opposite directions. Crimes, for example, which in Europe and America would be punished by penal servitude do not in China even cause shame; while *en revanche* conduct which in England would entail neither legal nor social penalty would in China be punishable with death. Suicide, which is so criminal in England as to bar Christian burial and cause juries to forswear themselves rather than return a true verdict, is publicly and officially extolled in China as the highest virtue. Results of moral evolution so disparate are not to be understood by rudely contrasting them and condemning off-hand the one extreme from the standpoint of its opposite. One would have to dig deep indeed into the foundations of the social structures to reach the point where the two civilisations would throw an intelligible light on each other; but it is by patient research and laborious sap rather than by head-breaking onslaughts on the outworks that the citadel of Chinese ethics is most likely to be carried. Hasty demonstrations may tend rather to consolidate the resistance than to overcome it.

Speaking generally, it is perhaps an open question whether under any conditions the moral improvement of mankind is furthered by denunciation. The more approved method surely is to build upon the existing foundation of what is good, and by stimulating the higher to gradually induce the neglect and atrophy of the baser qualities of the mind. Love succeeds where severity fails in leading individuals into virtuous paths; and the principle applied to the Chinese of diligently seeking out what is good in their hearts and in their practice, and of grafting on to it that which is of the same nature, but better, might result in a peaceful and happy transmutation. Such, however, is quite opposed to the system on which missionaries, as a body, seem now to work. They will hold no parley with " the enemy of souls."

To say, as in deed if not in words many of them do, that there is absolutely no good in systems which have sustained so great a people through periods of time during which the mightiest empires of the earth have risen, flourished, fallen, and been resolved into their elements is surely to do violence to obvious truth. And to assign all the good which cannot be gainsaid to the insidious devices of the Evil One is but a poor kind of monkish subterfuge, an escape for minds driven to the wall by fixed beliefs brought into open contradiction with observed facts.

In turning away, therefore, from the native virtues of the Chinese, the missionaries seem to be surrendering the strongest vantage ground they could occupy as a base for evangelising operations.

The dominating principle of Chinese life, that which rules the family and the nation, is universally admitted to be filial piety, the systematised reverence for living and dead parents. As to this the sages did nothing more than put the seal of their authority on a popular cult, which was already in their days of immemorial antiquity, the outward observances only having changed. There is probably in all the world no stronger moral principle, able as it is to command unlimited sacrifices from every living man and woman—to which the imperial service itself has to yield. Nothing can stand in the way of filial duty, whether it be to the living or the dead. It is one of the wonders of the world, as it certainly is the life of the Chinese nation. It deserves at least reasonable study. It links the living Chinaman to the whole past of his family and race, not by bonds of nebulous tradition, but in what he feels to be real living contact. It links him no less to the future, in which he shall live as the past lives in and about him. The custom of adoption, not peculiar to China, is one of the provisions which society has made to secure to every individual his due participation in the life to come.

Volumes might be written on the pros and cons of filial piety. The results are not all good by any means. The imperiousness of the one dominant principle seems to trample to extinction other principles which we Westerns deem equally important. Improvident marriages with their consequences, poverty and infanticide, may be carried to the adverse side of the account. Among the most commonly observed social results of the family solidarity, which is nothing but the constant expression of the filial principle, may be mentioned the continuous responsibility for family debts, which stands in such wide opposition to Western social ethics. A foreign house of business fails, owing large debts to Chinese, let us say, among others. The families of the debtors may be as rich as Crœsus, but it would be deemed an act of quixotic generosity for a son or a brother to indemnify the creditors. Conversely, a Chinese who should fail in like circumstances would entail the burden of his debt on his family and posterity. Active individual enterprise is promoted by the one principle, while caution and family supervision are ensured by the other; on which side lies the ultimate balance of good and evil it would be hard to estimate.

What then is the attitude of Christianity towards this venerable, deep-rooted moral force? Do the missionaries seek to attach it to their service? On the contrary, they refuse to tolerate it on the face of the earth,* and bluntly call on China to choose forthwith between Christ and her ancestors:—and she does.

* "I fear that if this motion is passed we are committed to the statement that there is nothing connected with ancestral worship which we can for a moment tolerate."—Rev. J. Ross, Shanghai Conference, 1891. [The motion *was* passed.]

As regards all such matters the missionaries seem to proceed on a regular and consistent plan. They take up a subject as a chemist does a substance in his laboratory, and they apply to it a very limited range of verbal tests. As soon as they find the blue precipitate corresponding to the word "idolatry" in their vocabulary the analysis is complete, and the phial is labelled and placed in a glass case for the instruction of future neophytes. Word-worship is the perpetual bane of the book-learned, who, like other men, become assimilated to what they work in, and end by putting the symbols in the place of the things symbolised. Missionaries seem to suffer from two forms of this disease of the learned. One is exhibited in an array of phrases transferred from archaic Hebrew and Aramaic Greek to archaic, but very beautiful English, which are in early youth committed blindly to memory, and in adult life worshipped, the little idols being kept neatly ranged in rows in little cerebral shrines, dusted and always ready to be brought out. The other form is the worship of words in general —logolatry.

Under the tyranny of this cultus a whole generation of missionaries have expended their strength in wearisome logomachy about the Chinese terms used for the Supreme. The Protestants could not, of course, employ the terms already made familiar to the Chinese by the early

Catholic missions, because theirs was the god of the hills, while ours was the god of the plains — or for some equally valid reason. During the thirty years' disputation it would be hard to say how many new word-deities may have been added to the Chinese Pantheon, but the dispute has ended in smoke. With better knowledge most of the Protestant missionaries are now unostentatiously adopting the term which was used by the early Jesuits. But what a sacrifice to mere words — "husks" as the late Dr. Williamson ventured to call them, to the scandal of his missionary brethren.

Such a word-idol is this "idolatry," which, being biblical, must be revered.* What is meant by it

---

* "Nor is it possible to estimate the harm which has been done in matters of higher speculation and conduct, by loose verbiage, though we may guess at it by observing the dislike which people show to have anything about their religion said to them in simple words,—for then they understand it. . . .

"Few passages of the book, which at least some part of the nations at present most advanced in civilisation accept as an expression of final truth, have been more distorted than those bearing on idolatry. For the idolatry there denounced is neither sculpture, nor veneration of sculpture. It is simply the substitution of an 'Eidolon,' phantasm or imagination of Good, for that which is real and enduring, from the Highest Living Good, which gives life, to the lowest material good which ministers to it. The Creator, and the things created which he is said to have 'seen good' in creating, are in this their eternal goodness appointed always to be worshipped—i. e., to have goodness and worth ascribed to them from the heart."—Ruskin.

E

in our modern days is no doubt the worship of something other than God—or, according to Mr. Hudson Taylor, who thinks in Hebrew, "Jehovah"—but as the missionaries perhaps know neither what is, nor what is not, God, they take a good deal upon them in pronouncing judgment in matters which transcend their comprehension. As was hinted by one of themselves, moreover, to apply to Chinese, whose sin is fidelity to their own traditions, a term coined to describe Hebrew renegades, is very like uttering counterfeit money. This word "idolatry" as used by missionaries is little more than something to conjure with, and Chinese ancestral "worship," as it is designated by them, will probably long withstand attack by paper swords of that kind. One learned member of the Shanghai Conference, some way gone in logolatry, formulated seventeen separate and compact verbal reasons for forbidding the "worship" of Chinese ancestors!

The Mohammedans, purer monotheists than the Christians, and being themselves Chinese, knowing the Chinese mind, have found means of accommodation with Chinese ancestoral worship; and so no doubt would the Chinese Christians also, if the missionaries would but trust a little to the natural operation of Christian affections in their hearts instead of affronting the whole nation by vehement denunciation of what is literally dearer to them than life; foreclosing the subject against future argument, and slamming the door against new light.*

The worship is open to the observation of everybody in China. All Souls' day, or the Spirits' Festival, occurs on the full of the seventh moon, which fell this year on the 19th August. Immense processions of men, women, and children on that day sally out of cities and villages dressed in white mourning robes to offer sacrifices at their family graves, and decorate them. Nor is the service confined to the family spirits. Close to the foreign settlement at one of the Treaty ports is a noticeably well-kept grave which is frequently visited by solitary Chinese. It is the tomb of a physician famous no less for his medical skill than for his benevolent character; and it is a regular practice of the people who live in the locality to bring incense to the grave and consult the spirit of the deceased worthy. On the annual festival strings of visitors, mostly women, pay their respects to the spirit of the good physician. In this service reverence is no doubt mixed up with expectation of favours, as is the case in all religious systems whatsoever.

Of the missionaries' relations to Buddhism it would be too long to tell. Nor is it necessary to

* "The title of his paper [Rev. Dr. Martin's 'Plea for Toleration'] is one that cannot be discussed by any Protestant body."—Rev. J. Hudson Taylor, Shanghai Conference, 1890.

say more than that it also, with all its superstitions and its benevolences, its great history and wonderful popularity, is simply abomination to be fought against till it is destroyed. For is it not also "idolatry"?*

Coming to the more positive side of the missionaries' teaching the evidence somewhat fails us, for excepting at the seaports, and in the case of the disciplined and regimented Catholics, the missionaries who are spread over China do pretty much what they individually like, and give such accounts of their work as they think sufficient.

Much as the division of the Christian force into so many separate factions is to be deplored, and detrimental to the prospects of the missions as is the transference of these relics of strife from their native homes to the soil of China, it is not on the missionaries but on the societies which send them out that the blame, if any, rests. That it is a great evil can hardly be doubted. Whenever Chinese converts obtain a hearing on the subject, they speak, with no ambiguity, of the immense loss of force which Christianity sustains through these divisions.

But there is perhaps a still more serious evil in the vagaries of hundreds of irresponsible evangelists who go about the country retailing the figments of their own excited brains as the pure

* "It is no sign of true religion to affront a false."—Rev. Dean Butcher, Shanghai Conference, 1877.

gospel. They say that whatever the diversities in their teaching may be they are at one with the main body in essentials; which is a mere begging of the question. How do they know what classification of "essentials" and "non-essentials" their ignorant hearers may be making? On these missionaries' own showing it is impossible to prevent the poor uneducated people from making of the whole thing a tangle of fetishism, nor do the evangelists always resist to the uttermost the tendency to make "medicine men" of them, which shows itself frequently in their ignorant followers. On all such matters, we repeat, we are dependent on the parties interested for information as to their doings, and as they are neither unbiassed, nor as a rule persons whose judgment has been strengthened by severe training, their statements have to be received with some caution. The most eccentric missionaries are naturally those, many of them single women, belonging to Mr. Hudson Taylor's China Inland Mission. They number 480, more than one-third of the total force of Protestant missionaries in China. They are drawn from every sect in England, from Canada, Sweden, and perhaps other countries; and the territory of China is systematically parcelled out among them so as to obviate collision and to minimise the outward aspect of their diversities of creed and conduct. Members of other bodies may look askance at the doings of the China Inland Mission as an English squire does at those of the Salvation Army, but they cannot dissociate themselves from them in the eyes of the Chinese, who make no fine-drawn distinctions where foreigners are concerned. It is not in the power of any missionary to limit his responsibility to his own personal work; he is bound in a moral partnership of unlimited liability, and his results can never be other than part of a general aggregate. He has no choice between tacitly endorsing all that every member of the missionary body does, and openly repudiating what he disapproves. But even his protests would not prevent his instruction being interpreted by the proceedings of others professing to teach the same doctrine.

The Inland missionaries are much given to street preaching and "itinerating," in which their unmarried women also take part, perambulating the streets of towns looking for invitations to enter houses. From their diaries and letters we get occasional glimpses of what these independent evangelists teach the Chinese. A species of thaumaturgy enters largely into their system. They here meet the Chinese on their own ground of spiritualism, and in cases of sickness or trouble, the missionaries are ready to back the foreign against the native Deity, after the manner of Elijah with the prophets of Baal. In other words, they live by prayer, not privately merely, but often openly, and by way of challenging their opponents. When a patient dies for whose recovery special prayer has been made, and the petitioners are self-pledged to a successful issue, they do not look at the material cause of death, but examine the mechanism of their prayer as if it were an experiment in physics that had miscarried. When they want a free passage in a steamboat they pray for it over-night, and the most hard-hearted shipping agent is unable to deny the naïvely-pious request preferred at 10 a.m. next day. Nothing of the most trivial kind happens to these good people but by miracle, that is to say, by special and continuous interpositions of the Almighty, with whose ideas they affect an easy familiarity which to minds reverentially constituted is rather shocking. Hence perhaps the very general prejudice against pietism which the pietists are too prone to attribute to the secular antagonism between good and evil, they having never a moment's doubt on which side of the line *they* stand! There is, however, no gainsaying the driving force of such epigrammatic convictions, and if the professors could only show moderately consistent success in drawing the fire from Heaven, they would inevitably supersede all the Chinese fortune-tellers, geomancers, doctors, and priests. Unluckily in the mere mundane vision of the Chinese the poor Inland missionaries are seen to be subject to all the common casualties of life just like other folks, and their appeal to unseen compensations for earthly griefs satisfies only the few who come within the incandescent sphere of their direct personal attraction.

The discipline which the missionaries attempt to enforce on their converts is, like their teaching, varied. Nearly everywhere, among Protestants Sabbatarianism is insisted upon, which to a Chinaman, isolated in the crowd and struggling for a living, is a test of faith difficult to be imagined by people whose birthright is a seventh-day rest. There are, however, many missionaries who perceive the hardship, and are not convinced of the authority for the obligation, and who consequently relax somewhat the severe Sabbatarian *régime*.

There are some again who deny the Communion to Chinese who drink or smoke, even common tobacco; and nearly, if not quite all, refuse the Sacraments to those who touch opium. There is not, of course, a shadow of authority scriptural, patristic, or ecclesiastical, for any of these prohibitions; nothing but the self-sufficing judgment of the missionaries.* This opens a wide vista of possible abuse in the future as the borders of the Christian community become enlarged.

Nor is it Chinese vices properly so called which

---

* "*Sabbath observance, opium smoking, ancestral worship, &c.* . . . I think we should teach the native Christians from the Scripture, and allow them to legislate on these points. Let them be chiefly responsible. We are not called upon to legislate."—Rev. Dr. Edkins, at Shanghai Conference, 1877.

alone incur the reprobation of the missionaries. Societies whose bond of union is abstinence from flesh, alcohol, opium, tobacco, and impurity, and whose members are held strictly to their rules, are under the ban of the missionaries—always, let it be understood, with most significant exceptions.* They pronounce such kind of abstinence " idolatry," a verdict always ready to hand which saves troublesome examination. The Chinese are, in fact, worshipping their own virtue—which no missionary ever does—and trusting to their own efforts instead of—&c., &c.

One practice which seems to be most obnoxious to the missionaries of certain sections is vegetarianism, which is rather common in China. This, it appears, is one of the subtlest wiles of the Devil, to make the Chinese simulate goodness even before the arrival of the missionaries, and accordingly the victims of this deadly delusion must be saved, from their vegetarian diet at least, if not entirely from the vegetarian superstition. A single breach of the vow is all that is required to destroy the accumulated merit of half a life-time; and the missionaries naïvely relate the snares they set for

* " These sections of the population [the religious sects] are of the highest importance. They seem the only people in the empire alive to any sense of spiritual realities, ' the only living sinners in the empire,' as I once called them. . . They have many affinities to divine truth, and are earnestly groping after more light."—Rev. Dr. Williamson, at Shanghai Conference, 1890.

these pseudo-virtuous people to entrap them into transgression. The breaking of an egg, innocent as it looks, is sometimes the means blessed to this end; and we read of wily old converts laying earnest siege to new inquirers in order that by some means they may be seduced into eating pork in their company—a sort of equivalent of " taking the shilling."

Such are some specimens of the excrescences of the new Christianity which is being planted in China. These lie on the surface of the missionary periodicals, but probably an independent inquirer among their stations in the interior would discover a world of other matters, novel to him, which have become too commonplace for the missionaries themselves to think of recording.

The various schemes of theology, which are taught to the Chinese, Japanese, and other Eastern peoples would require a separate treatise, and much more information than is at present available to the public to elucidate. It may be stated, generally, that modern biblical criticism is simply ignored, as well as the widening tendency of the modern churches in matters of set doctrine. Men who landed in China 30 or 40 years ago, with a complete outfit of cut-and-dried opinions, have naturally been too busy to change them, unless they happen to possess the rare faculty for assimilating new ideas, which even the Chinese life itself suggests to some open minds. Thackeray tells us of a certain German gentleman who passed his youth in the English army in the Georgian era, and who when found by a traveller fifty years later buried in his native principality, spoke a dialect of English which consisted mainly of oaths, grown out of date in good society, but which were found bottled up and seemingly quite fresh in the memory of this veteran. Theology *in partibus* seems to be in a somewhat similar case, and it is curious sometimes to come across in the Far East antiquated samples of creeds which are disappearing in the lands of their origin, just as one finds in old Dutch houses specimens of the Chinese porcelain of the seventeenth century. While even the cast-iron theologians of the Free Church of Scotland and the stern Presbyterians of America are seeking ways of escape from the rigid fetters in which the famous Westminster divines have bound them these 200 years and more, and are actually making concessions to unbaptised infants, Calvinism in its naked form is being diligently inculcated on Chinese and Japanese, as if it were the ultimate and indisputable truth. A zealous evangelist of those parts in conversation lately frankly made this confession:—The Almighty [may the irreverence be forgiven!] having got into a legal difficulty with mankind, devised a plan by which the penalty due should be imposed on another who was innocent of offence. By this means the human race was to be saved, or at least rendered salvable.

Other complications, however, prevented the consummation of the Divine scheme, and in fact only a select few were ever really intended to participate in the so-dearly-purchased redemption. In order, however, that the condemned, by far the larger portion of mankind, might be technically put in the wrong, they were to be given a chance of hearing the Gospel, which they were foredoomed to reject; and their final condemnation was thereby rendered more terrible than if there had been no scheme of redemption at all, or they had never heard of it. But the important thing was that God should be justified, and even get glory!

So little have these hide-bound creeds advanced in a century that Burns's caricature of them is as applicable as when he wrote:

> "O Thou wha in the Heavens dost dwell,
> Wha as it pleases best thysel',
> Sends ane to Heaven and ten to Hell
> A' for thy glory:
> An' no for ony gude or ill
> They've done afore Thee!"

A lady, fresh perhaps from some theological seminary, propounds for "Chinese women"—women who, on the testimony of another experienced and keen-witted missionary lady, are unable to grasp the simplest abstract idea—a scheme of divinity so elaborate that if the salvation of our bishops were made conditional on their mastering it, the majority of their lordships would have sorrowfully to accept the alternative.

The crop of doctrinal anomalies exhibited in a country where each individual utters recklessly whatever comes into his head, without check either from higher authority or from public opinion—that of the natives being of course disregarded—is, as might be expected, a rank jungle growth the extent of which can never be known. Hints may occasionally be gathered from the printed papers circulated by missionaries among the heathen of a very chaos of creeds, without so much as a sect to stand sponsor for them. One man, for example, issues a leaflet which laboriously proves that the cosmos was not created by God, as is commonly believed, but by Jesus. Christian worship is, by the same unreason, shown to be directed to Jesus, and *not to God,* an essential distinction being made between them. It is not surprising, after this, to find the corollary of justification by faith worked for all it is worth by some of the irresponsible apostles, ridden by a kind of quack logic, who lay it down plainly to the Chinese that Christians need not be moral, as they have only to believe!

What the general effect on the Chinese of these varied and eccentric teachings may be we have no means of knowing. But it is obvious to enquire whether, though Christianity may nominally gain by the untrammelled zeal of zealots of all kinds, it must not eventually pay the penalty of being found out as an imposition?

In matters of material improvement the Chinese and Japanese are not treated so. They are not first given wooden ships, muzzle-loading guns, or the Ptolemaic system of the heavens, but the result of the very latest discoveries in every branch of science; the latest excursions into the regions of thought, and the newest things in sociology. Why should they be so largely denied the like advantages in the sphere of religion?

It requires, perhaps, some other eye than that of a working missionary to perceive the danger to the future of Christianity from a too rigid adherence to wordy things which are beginning to fall away from the religion of the West like withered leaves that have served their temporary purpose. The light of literature will not be stayed in the Far East any more than it has been in India, and when the Chinese discover, as their Japanese neighbours are already doing, and as the Indians did before them, that the thing which was given them as Christianity would not stand the light which was brought to bear upon it, they will be apt to throw it over, and accept the teaching of the missionaries with the religious ingredient carefully filtered out. As regards the old countries of Christendom, there is much to be said for the gradual and guarded infusion of expanding views of truth, lest the new wine should crack the old skins; and the officers of religion in those countries may be pardoned for maintaining forms even after they have lost some of their meaning. But the like excuse does not cover the introduction into new countries of doctrinal forms which, if not already obsolete elsewhere, are fast becoming so. The missionaries come to uproot the religions of the Chinese in order to offer them something infinitely better, but between the people's appreciation of that something better and their present apprehension of the destructive force that menaces them there is a very wide gulf, in the passage of which the best hopes of the friends of China may founder. It behoves the missionaries to look well to it that at least no worn-out simulacrum of Christianity is offered, to the prejudice of a purer presentment of it which may follow.

Perhaps what is really vital in Christianity, that which has kept it alive through every variety of form, and carried it even through seas of crime perpetrated in its name, has never yet been presented in a pure form anywhere. Perhaps the constitution of human nature will always prevent the true essence from being isolated from its grosser concomitants; but at any rate the higher ideal which is coming more clearly into view in Christendom might be more aimed at than it has yet been in China. And as one would not go into action carrying lumber which must be thrown away at the first encounter, so missionaries might with permanent profit to their sacred cause consider how much of their old (and new) religious furniture it is necessary for them to bring into the China campaign.

A real difficulty begins to be felt also with regard to the Bible itself. The book, as such, is held in such superstitious regard by the text-ridden masses that the most strenuous efforts have been made to circulate its contents everywhere, and more especially in literary China. Where the missionaries could not penetrate the book could be sent, and where they might provoke opposition by their bodily presence the Scriptures might be quietly studied in chambers with much hope of future harvest. Till lately not a doubt was breathed as to the absolute wisdom of this procedure, but the unloosing of one tongue led to the unloosing of many, and at the last Conference in Shanghai the propriety of the indiscriminate circulation of the Bible, without note or comment, was freely canvassed. It was an unpleasant discovery, after thirty years of work at high pressure, to find that when the harvest was looked for, tares—nay brambles and baleful weeds—instead of wheat had covered the ground. Of the possibility of such a result the blasphemous uses to which the Tai-ping Rebels turned the Old and New Testaments might have afforded the missionaries some warning. But they seem to have gone on wholly unaware what effect the Bible was producing on the minds of the thousands into whose hands it had been put. They simply did their plain duty and left the consequences to take care of themselves, or, as they prefer to phrase it, the results were in God's hands. The more thoughtful heads—and it required some courage for them to say so—now recognise that the Bible is not a proper book to be indiscriminately read by people quite unprepared for its teachings, and out of sympathy with its spirit. They have seen that the foulest attacks made against Christianity by the Chinese *literati* are loaded to the muzzle with missiles from the Bible, which is a perfect arsenal of weapons to be used against the missionary cause. The seed which is wafted far and wide on the wind cannot be controlled, nor can the soil into which it falls be either selected or tended. The hard things in the Bible which stagger thoughtful youths at home, though familiarised with them from earliest infancy, produce startling effects on the minds of those who have no teacher to explain and no mother to cover them with the gentle authority of her love.

How little some of the missionaries feel the need of smoothing down the less digestible portions of the Old Testament may be seen from their selecting some of the hardest passages for special advertisement. Their tracts, for example, which are intended to be read by Chinese who have never heard a foreigner's voice, are coarsely illustrated by such scenes as Jonah being

If it be remarked by some readers that scant appreciation has been in these pages expressed either of the men engaged, or in the work of the missions, the reply is that a panegyric would have been easy and pleasant to write, since the materials for it abound. But there is a time for everything, and it seemed more to the present purpose to endeavour to discover how far the anti-Christian feeling in China might fairly be traced to the proceedings of Christian missionaries. Again, it may be objected, and with good reason, that the present essay is but the criticism of a *dilettante* on the serious work of serious men; to which the only answer is that as an urchin sitting on a gate may see when the hounds are at fault, and as staff-officers in the field may sometimes get hints from country-folk who are innocent of strategy, so may those who are wiser than the writer extract some useful intelligence even from the lucubrations of a layman.

Yet, to prevent misconstruction, a word ought perhaps still to be said concerning the quality of the Chinese Christian converts. Few as they may be, when all told, and mixed as they must be with spurious professors, it is a gratifying fact, which cannot be gainsaid, that Christians of the truest type, men ready to become martyrs, which is easy, and who lead "helpful and honest" lives, which is as hard as the ascent from Avernus, crown the labours of the missionaries, and have done so from the very beginning. It is thus shown that the Christian religion is not essentially unadapted to China, and that the Chinese character is susceptible to its regenerating power. The road to the Chinese conscience, therefore, having once been found, the prospect of an abundant entrance thereto might be considered hopeful, were it not for such drawbacks as those which have been above referred to. The danger is that while one is attracted, ten, nay a hundred, others may be repelled without arousing misgivings in the missionary mind; so that even present successes may be purchased at the cost of heavy future reverses. Such possibilities the ordinary working missionary, intent at all hazards on gathering in his own sheaves, can hardly be expected to entertain. The more need, therefore, that those who are interested in the subject, but are under no strain to produce a daily tale of bricks, should venture on the wider survey, and get the clearest view possible of the general drift of the movement.

Among the "hindrances" which figure so largely in missionary discussions it seems scarcely yet to have occurred to any one that the chief of all hindrances to the spread of Christianity in China is the missionaries themselves. Wise old Dr. Nevius dared to say, in full Conference, that "the Bible-sellers, so far from paving the way for the missionary may, on the contrary, obstruct it;" and it would be producing the line of thought but one swallowed by the great fish, and Jael in the act of driving her tent-peg through the temples of her sleeping guest. These things of course present no real difficulty to the acceptance of the Chinese, who are perfectly ready to swallow Jonah and the whale too, if the fish be big enough. The physiological problem which the prophet had to solve during the next few days is mere child's play beside the thousand and one wonders which fill the imaginations of every Oriental people. Nor is the treachery of Jael calculated to shock Chinese notions of honest reprisal. But whether Christianity is much assisted by such rough forms of introduction is quite another question.

The effect of the mere translation is probably difficult enough to appraise accurately, but there need be no difficulty in perceiving—what, however, has had to be brought home to the missionaries by the rudest proofs—that men of a strange race, predisposed to be hostile, and not over-nice in their imaginations, were not at all certain to find edification either in the biographies or the anacreontics of the Bible. To refer only to one instance: What is an educated heathen likely to make of the evidence of the central truth of Christianity, the miraculous birth, as presented to him for the first time in the New Testament? What the Chinese *literati* do make of it the missionaries know very well, and have known for a long time, though few dare speak out.

It so happens that, impure as the Chinese imagination may be, the whole body of their classical literature does not contain a single passage which needs to be slurred over or explained away, and which may not be read in its full natural sense by youth or maiden. And to people nurtured on a literature so immaculate in these respects there are things in the Bible which are calculated to create a prejudice against its teachings, even in well-disposed minds.

The question was argued out at the Shanghai Conference, but it would be useless to follow the discussion in detail. One argument may be worth quoting for its typical significance. It was that of Dr. Wright, delegate of the British and Foreign Bible Society, and it amounted to this, that to doubt the propriety of forcing the whole Bible on the Chinese was to question the infallibility of Wycliffe and Luther!—perhaps of the B. and F. B. S. itself.

Committees are now discussing new versions, and Bible Societies are in friendly rivalry respecting them, while perhaps the wiser scheme of restricting the circulation and keeping it under greater supervision has not received adequate consideration. The Roman Catholics in China, as elsewhere, have shown great circumspection in the issue of the Scriptures. They consider that strong meat is not for babes, whether in the West or East.

stage further to suggest that the missionary, in his turn, may also be obstructing. Will the coming generation, while profiting by the arduous labours of their predecessors, be able also to clear the obstacles created for them by the generation which is passing away? That is a serious and also a practical question.

May not the missionaries who are apt to trace the hand of Providence in everything * recognise something of it even in this—that the Christianisation of China is waiting for men of simple faith, little concerned about themselves or their systems, ready to honour the good wherever found, who will leave the windmills called "strongholds of Satan" severely alone, and unobtrusively seek entrance to the hearts of living men—waiting in short for the time when Christianity can be introduced to the great Chinese people in a form that will be permanent in proportion as it is pure?

* "China is the most difficult missionary field in the world, and therefore, to human calculation, the most hopeless. This, I think, is the reason why God, when rekindling the missionary spirit in His Church, allowed China to be so long closed against missionary effort."—Rev. Dr. Talmage, at Shanghai Conference, 1877.

III. MODUS VIVENDI.

To recapitulate :—

I.—The missionaries are placed and maintained in China by foreign force coercing the Chinese Government.

II.—The Government of China, humiliated before its subjects by the Treaties imposed on it, is made further odious by protecting, under external pressure, the foreign missions, against the sense of the people.

III.—The propaganda has, over the whole country, aroused the hatred of the people, and the feeling shows no outward sign of abatement.

IV.—Proselytising success has been hindered by these causes, as well as by the combative form under which the foreign religion itself has been presented.

What then is the outlook?

For the Chinese Government: perpetual foreign coercion.

For the Chinese nation: an incessant ferment of angry passions, and a continuous education in ferocity against Christianity.

For the foreign missionaries: pillage and massacre at intervals followed by pecuniary indemnification, an indefinite struggle with the hatred of a whole nation; compensated by a certain number of genuine converts to their faith.

There may be fanatical and one-idea'd missionaries who glory in the prospect of strife, and count persecution the crowning testimony to their fidelity. But the moderate men, constituting (it may be hoped) the larger proportion, know better. They make an honest distinction between martyrdom and suffering for mere folly and recklessness. And to such it must be a matter of sad reflection, at the end of thirty years of active missionary work in the interior of China, that the people should be up in arms against them, and that the prospects of propagandism are actually worse now than they were at the beginning of that period.

As all the parties concerned in this question are sharing, in their different ways, in the misery of the present situation, they might all, one would think, be disposed to consider any means available for the amelioration of the evils that press upon them. As regards the two principal parties to the conflict, the missionaries and the Chinese officials and people, matters have been allowed to go too far to hope for any voluntary reconciliation between them. For were even the provoking cause removed the cooling process in racial or national animosities is slow, and subject to reactions. Nothing short of a miracle indeed could be expected to undo in a century the bitterness which has been fomenting for a generation. But the provoking cause cannot be removed. The missionaries cannot cease their operations, even during a truce, and the irritation which their mere presence excites must therefore be kept up, with what fresh exacerbation of feeling the history of the next twenty years will perhaps show.

Any hope of relieving the tension is more likely to be found in the deliberations of the different governments than either in modification of the tactics of the propaganda or in change in the sentiments of the people. And the foreign governments have every inducement to seek some safer *modus vivendi* than exists at present. Formerly, indeed, some of them might be interested in missionary troubles as affording them convenient occasions to intervene for their own purposes; but the quasi-protectorate of Christians, which never had a true legal basis, has in these later days been virtually dissolved, and its political value lost, by being shared in by all the Powers.

It may be assumed, therefore, that the Western Powers would unanimously desire to see the missionary question so disposed of as that it might never again become a subject of even diplomatic correspondence; while to the Chinese Government it would be worth millions of money to have this dangerous rock taken out of the way.

As we have seen, the two aspects of Christianity —not affecting its principles, but merely incidental to its form of presentation—which render it odious to the Chinese are: its foreign agents, and its maintenance by foreign arms. The one cannot be got rid of, unless indeed the Chinese were to show the same interest in Christianity as they once did in Buddhism, and send their own missionaries to the West to bring in the new religion. The other, being a creation of the foreign treaties, may by treaty be undone.

Were the alliance of the Christian missions with the military power of the West to be brought to an end a chief root of bitterness would doubtless be extracted from the Chinese mind, and a basis might then be established for gradually improving the relations between the people and the foreign missions. And though at first sight this might seem to imply an abandonment of teachers and converts to the fury of their enemies, yet the altered *status* would not be without its compensations to both classes.

If the scheme of protection which is based on existing treaties could be relied upon to be always maintained in effective operation there would be no need for seeking any other. Were any one or more of the Western Powers consistent in their armed support of missions, never relaxing their pressure on the Chinese Government; and were the Chinese Government on its part possessed in reality of its full nominal authority over all sections of its people, it is conceivable that the *literati* and provincial mobs might be first over-awed, then subdued, and finally conciliated. For there is nothing like utter and unmistakable defeat for securing the good will of the Chinese. In all cases where foreign force has been actually resorted to it has been perfectly successful in establishing peace. The English raid on the turbulent and piratical villages near Swatow about twenty-five years ago, though scarcely justified on its legal merits, not only gave a peace to the neighbourhood which has endured to this day, but it has converted a population of brigands and murderers into orderly and prosperous citizens; and in short has civilised a large district which the native authorities were never able properly to control. The firmness shown in 1868 in dealing with certain outrages on missionaries at Yangchow by the British Consul, the late Sir W. Medhurst, backed by that gallant old seaman, Sir Harry Keppel, converted that from being the most dangerous into one of the safest of mission stations. There has been no exception to the rule, that the strong hand has never failed to give peace and disperse ill-feeling.

The drawback to that mode of procedure is its spasmodic and uncertain operation. Once in twenty years perhaps the Western Powers may gird themselves up for a forcible remonstrance with China, but this phase of the business is like a storm which slowly gathers to a head, and either bursts or passes, leaving the scene much as it was before. How often in a century is it reasonable to hope that England, France, and Germany, to say nothing of Russia and the United States, could be brought to take concerted action, as they have done recently, in China? A war in Europe, for example, caused the worst outrage ever perpetrated by the Chinese on foreigners, the Tientsin massacre of 1870, to be passed over with scarcely any notice by the Powers concerned. And what is to happen in the long intervals of inaction, when the Western governments forget the very existence of China? The removal of pressure which immediately follows each demonstration affords, by the natural law of reaction, fresh encouragement to the disaffected, and from the day after one settlement of grievances is concluded a new accumulation begins, if not in the identical spots where reparation may have been exacted, in a hundred other places. It will be extremely interesting to observe in the next few years the attitude of the populations in the Yangtze valley who have been mulcted to pay the cost of their recent riotings.

The action of Western governments is liable, moreover, to be weakened by other considerations besides the effects of mere apathy or pre-occupation. While vindicating or desiring to vindicate the rights of their own nationals they are liable to be visited by qualms of doubt as to the propriety of their proceedings in particular cases as they arise. They know their data to be incomplete, and mixed and contradictory accounts reach them as to the relations between the Chinese Imperial Government and its subordinate governments, and between these latter and the *literati* and people. It has been observed also on critical occasions during the past quarter of a century that the Western governments are accessible to the private representations of persons speaking with authority (though not always with responsibility) on Chinese matters, while the reports of their own accredited agents are comparatively neglected. It is not, therefore, difficult to imagine how, before deciding on forcible measures in any particular case, the resolution of foreign governments may be in danger of being paralysed by misgivings of various kinds.

And there are unquestionably real difficulties on the Chinese side also. It is easy to point to treaties and demand their strict fulfilment; easy also to point out the inconsistency or duplicity of a government whose public proclamations pass unheeded in the country. Duplicity is the universal resource of the weak in dealing with the strong. But statesmen who feel the difficulties of good and just government pressing on themselves must also take account of the difficulties which are peculiar to the governments with which they have dealings;

and the history of foreign intercourse with China, while it proves the efficacy of force, shows also that force has been resorted to on occasions when perhaps a better acquaintance with the true state of the case might have obviated it.

In the recent crisis, if indeed it can be properly considered as past, the difficulties of the central Government were of no imaginary kind. Sudden explosions at numerous points covering an immense tract of country called for great circumspection; careful sifting of reports from all sides was necessary in order to get a practical appreciation of the forces at work, and their direction. Rash ill-informed action might have had dangerous results. It was not necessarily the connection of foreigners with the riots that caused the hesitation, for the instinctive caution of the Chinese Government is shown quite as much in matters of purely domestic concern. The governments, imperial and provincial, are weak enough, or wise enough, to court their proletariat, and it is not uncommon to see the most powerful rulers cowed by popular demonstrations, even of very moderate calibre. There were special reasons for circumspection in dealing with the outbreaks of May, for as has since been shown, the focus of the insubordination was the turbulent province of Hunan, and it so happened that the troops and the officers at the disposal of the Government on the Yangtze were all drawn from that province. An insurrection of the people, or mutiny of the troops, would have served the ends of the Western governments as little as those of the Chinese Government itself.

Hunan prides itself on being the cradle of patriotism, and the impregnable citadel of conservatism in China. It has given to the State some of its greatest men, and has supplied the army with its best soldiers. The province has for these and other reasons, and by force of character, exercised almost a dominant influence in the counsels of the empire. It has been a tradition that none but a native of Hunan could be Viceroy of Nanking, because the troops and crews of gunboats, &c., employed within the provinces under that government, being Hunanese, would not obey a stranger. The rule was broken through this year, in the appointment of a non-Hunanese to the acting viceroyalty of the lower Yangtze, and the recent outbreaks are believed to be some of the consequences. The attitude of the Hunanese towards foreigners has always been one of the fiercest hostility. They refuse to receive any foreign inventions even, and have defied the Government itself to erect a telegraph line through the province. Taking him all round, probably the greatest statesman China has produced in this century was Tsêng Kwo-fan, the father of the late Marquis Tsêng, of an old Hunan family. It will illustrate at once the truculent bearing of the Hunanese towards foreigners, and the supremacy of the populace in China, to relate what happened to that most popular of all the high officials of his day or since. Tsêng Kwofan, then Viceroy of Chihli, was ordered by the Imperial Government to proceed to Tientsin—his own provincial capital being Pao-ting-Fu, four days' journey into the interior—to investigate the causes of the Tientsin massacre of 21st June, 1870. He reported, awarded certain reparation, found a number of people guilty of murder, and beheaded them. Foreigners did not think the settlement altogether adequate, and in particular they were convinced that the true ringleaders were let off because they were influential, while certain individuals of no reputation were delivered in their stead for execution. The Hunanese took a different view, and to mark their contempt for their great fellow-provincial's truckling to foreigners, they struck his name off the roll of the Hunan Club in Peking, defaced his tablet there, and did him further dishonour. The Viceroy felt all this acutely, but though he spared neither money nor other conciliatory appliances it was only after a length of time and with the greatest difficulty that he succeeded in wiping out the outward signs of his disgrace. It may be further mentioned in this connection that the late Marquis Tsêng himself, when he returned from Europe, dared not visit his ancestral home because he was held by his countrymen to have been defiled by his residence among foreigners, and was apprehensive of a rough reception in his native province. The populace did actually burn down his house to stigmatise his defection from the anti-foreign traditions of Hunan. Other provinces are only in a less degree, and less aggressively, anti-foreign than Hunan itself. The sacred province, however, considers it has special grounds for its pre-eminence in anti-foreign feeling in the capture and exile of the Canton Viceroy, Yeh, by the English in 1858, he being a distinguished native of Hunan. But was it not rather the foreign hatred which he had imbibed there with his mother's milk that led Yeh into the course of conduct which precipitated his fall?

These defiant populations might be reduced to discipline, and even tamed into amiability, by a moderate use of force, as was the no less unruly population of Canton under the firm hand of Sir Harry Parkes, who governed that city after its capture by foreign troops in 1858. But the decisive stroke and the firm hand are just what are usually wanting to the Chinese Government, whose fixed policy in all matters concerning the people is a temporising one. Nothing probably would have been more convenient to the Government during the recent crisis than that some foreign power should have taken the law into its own hands, quelled the riots and punished the rioters. A raid on Hunan at the present moment would be a god-send to the poor Viceroy, whose authority has been openly trampled on. He could then turn to his people and say: "This is what comes of your turbulence, and now I shall have to come and take the foreign devils off your back," whereby great *kudos* would have come to him, whereas now he has to pull his own chestnuts off the hob by Imperial command.

It is, perhaps, an open question whether, considering the timid and dilatory disposition of the Chinese Government, and the way the evil-disposed people have of taking advantage of it, the hands of the Government are not strengthened by the pressure put upon them by foreigners to compel them to keep order in their own country. As a hypothetical parallel let us once more recall the case of the Government of India in 1856–7. Supposing that the excitement of the population of Hindostan had been directed not against the Government, but against some third party which the Government was bound by treaty to protect, is it not conceivable that, spurred by the demands of such third party, or even by a sheer sense of obligation, Lord Canning might have brushed aside the Calcutta Secretaries, the Hallidays, Beadons, and all the obfuscated old colonels, and adopted such drastic measures as would have stamped out the conflagration in its earlier stages, and so saved the mutiny? As often as not the luckiest things men or nations do are the things that are forced upon them. Such a hypothesis, far fetched as applied to British India, has a true bearing on the circumstances of China, for side by side with the aversion to foreigners there is manifestly a spirit of active disaffection towards the Government itself, among the disbanded soldiery, disappointed scholars, and the needy classes generally; and both animosities are served by the same outbreaks. By the disabling of one limb of the coalition through the timely coercion of foreign powers, the combined movement would be crippled. This is a view of the matter, however, which has only a speculative interest, as no such considerately calculated action will ever be taken.

It is generally easy after the event to discern what ought to or might have been done, but in the obscurity of a crisis errors are only too likely to be made in every country; and where it is such a complex case as that of one or more Powers employing irresistible force to compel another to coerce its own people, with a very imperfect comprehension of the conditions of the problem, the disposition to evade or postpone action will be on all ordinary occasions overpowering; and thus the protection due to the foreign residents * in China is always liable to be rendered nugatory in the very attempt to translate it into practice.

The protection of missionaries in China, against the national will, by the strong arm, whether of

* The Chinese animosity is not confined to missionaries, although they, as pioneers, chiefly bear the brunt of it.

foreign powers or of the native Government, being thus shown to be at the best uncertain and inadequate, the question naturally arises whether the status of the missions admits of such modifications as would make it possible for the Government to do justice to them without encountering the secret opposition of its own people.

From consideration of the difficulty, so often proved, of following a consistent and dignified line of policy, under existing circumstances, we opine that the Western Powers would be inclined to welcome any solution of this perennial missionary question which would relieve them from the responsibility of protecting the missionaries in China, a duty which they can only fulfil in a capricious and defective manner. And if the right which has been exercised is not one clearly laid down by any treaty provision it would be the more easy to modify existing relations by some new definition. In exchange for the withdrawal of the heavy hand of the Western Powers China would no doubt be willing to grant substantial concessions, extending even to the taking of Christianity under the shelter of the Imperial wing; as is virtually done with the other two foreign religions; and to the offering of satisfactory guarantees for the safety of the missionaries as well as of their native followers. Dr. Edkins indeed considers (see paper read at the last Shanghai Conference) that Christianity is already openly acknowledged by the State, and is nominally one of the established religions. Nor could any Edict of Nantes be more satisfactory as a charter of toleration than the Memorial to the Throne of the Tsung-li Yamên published in the *Peking Gazette* of 26th July, 1891, and the Imperial Rescript on that Memorial (see Appendix II.). The question then recurs, with accumulating urgency, what is it that hinders the theoretical from becoming practical? This enquiry always brings us back to the causes of the popular ill-will, and how far these causes are removable; for if such as are removable were actually removed there would be, as observed already, a way opened for discussing the deeper elements of the question. It might be possible, for example, by some general agreement among the missionaries, so to regulate such transactions as the acquisition of property, the building of churches in the interior, and other matters of a sumptuary nature as that some approach to conciliation might be made. These questions could be treated without touching any of those purely religious issues regarding which the missionaries are justifiably tenacious. And were these outside matters fairly removed from the arena of controversy an approach might be made to those more delicate questions, such as the conduct of schools, hospitals, &c., which touch both sides so tenderly. So long as things go on as at present suspicion will never be allayed as to the uses to which foreigners put such institutions.

An essential condition of a good working understanding between missionaries and the Chinese people would be the placing of the whole missionary establishments under official supervision. Personal visitation would have to be made obligatory on the local magistrates as part of their official routine, and they would be called upon to make regular reports to the chief authorities of their respective provinces. In this manner the utmost publicity would be given to missionary operations; no one would need to ask who are these people, and what do they do? and the familiar "half brick" which is kept ready to throw at strangers might gradually fall out of use. The Christian religion might thus obtain a real status in the country as well as enjoy the official recognition of the Government. Naturally, all inflammatory placards and calumnious brochures would have to be rigorously suppressed (as they have occasionally been before) and a general principle of give-and-take be introduced which would spread like oil over the angry waves.

A serious proposal to place foreign missionaries on a smooth working basis was made twenty years ago, and by the Chinese Government itself—almost the only example of true initiative with which it can be credited. The Tientsin massacre of June, 1870, and the disagreeable consequences which followed, impressed the Emperor's Ministers with the necessity of doing something to prevent future occurrences of the same kind; and the most liberal, fair, and open-minded Minister that has ever been in the Foreign Board, Wênseang, who was then in power, drew up for the consideration of the foreign governments the famous " Missionary Circular " of 1871.* It consisted of an elaborate and moderately expressed review of the whole position, followed by eight rules for the government of missionary relations with the people and officials in the provinces. The rules referred to (1) the management of orphanages, which it was proposed either to close altogether, or to place under severe restrictions; (2) the mixed attendance of women and men at public worship which, being contrary to Chinese propriety, scandalised the people; (3) the legal status of missionaries in the interior and the evil consequences of the *imperia in imperio* which had resulted through the missionaries separating themselves, and even their native converts, from the jurisdiction of the local authorities; (4) the restriction of proceedings in the case of riots to the persons actively participating in the same; (5) the clear definitions of passports so that missionaries should not be able to move about at will leaving no trace; (6) the need of strict examination into the character and antecedents of converts; (7) the etiquette to be observed

* Blue Book, " China No. 3, 1871.'

by missionaries in intercourse with officials, the missionaries not to arrogate official style; and (8) the reclamation of alleged sites of ancient churches to be stopped, great injustice having been done to Chinese through being obliged to surrender properties which they had honestly bought and paid for.

All these suggested rules were illustrated by specific instances of the evils resulting from the absence of such rules, and the whole document was based on the earnest desire of the Government that the foreign and native Christians should live in friendship with their Chinese neighbours.

The communication was not enthusiastically received by any of the foreign governments, although the good intentions of the Chinese Government were frankly acknowledged; and several of the charges made, in all good faith, against the missionaries were resented as untrue. The Tsungli Yamên no doubt failed to completely grasp the situation, and indeed the Ministers expressly stated that their circular only covered a small part of the ground, but at the same time, as the one honest attempt yet made to arrive at a *modus vivendi* it deserves honourable mention on the present occasion.

Fresh proposals in somewhat the same sense have been made by the Chinese Government during the recent discussions respecting redress for the outrages on the Yangtze in 1891; but the foreign diplomatic representatives naturally refused to entertain any suggestions of the sort until complete satisfaction had been given for these outrages.

The time may yet come, however, for considering some scheme of reconciliation between the opposing parties. And as the Circular of 1871 was addressed primarily to the missionaries of the Church of Rome—as the Governments of Great Britain and the United States were prompt to discover—so any hope of even a partial trial of a new agreement must still rest mainly on the Roman Catholic missions. They possess a solidarity which Protestant missions lack; they are under a strict *régime*; they have superiors whom they must obey and who can speak for them; and above all they possess in the present head of their Church the most far-sighted, the most liberal, and the most Christian-spirited Pontiff that has ever sat in the chair of St. Peter; who has shown himself at once tender and courageous; and is deeply solicitous for the welfare of the Church, expressly including in that definition Christians of every sect throughout the world.

Nor is the feeling of a coming change in the status of the missions altogether new to the Catholic fathers. The subject has in fact been a good deal discussed during the last few years, since the imperfect protectorate claimed by France was seen to be crumbling into dust. One missionary at least has expressed himself in no ambiguous terms on this point (see Appendix I.). The *rapprochement* between the Vatican and the Imperial court in 1886 on the occasion of the expropriation of the P'ei-tang Cathedral in Peking, opened the way to ulterior negotiations, and showed that there was no insuperable obstacle on either side to a purely ecclesiastical representation of the Catholic missions in Peking taking the place of a halting and half-hearted political one. Whether the views then exchanged have gathered consistency during the subsequent interval of incubation we are not aware, but the incidents of the present year have no doubt served to bring the question to the recollection of those interested.

From the point of view of living on neighbourly terms with the natives also the Catholic missions possess some clear advantages over their Protestant rivals. For one thing they are no longer such eager proselytisers as they were, but in several provinces at least, live in settled communities of Christians, where having planted churches, many of them already venerable, they now water, and watch for the increase.

In the matter of landowning, on the other hand, they are probably greater offenders than the Protestants. The Catholic fathers have not only an eye to the best sites—witness the Cathedrals at Canton and Pekin, the "Hills" near Shanghai and many other places—but they enter moreover into investments in real estate as a means of providing revenue—chiefly, however, at the Treaty ports. Their *procureurs* are excellent managers, and among their tenantry they are the most popular of landlords. So by their admirable economies they are able to supplement the subsidies of their missions, and whereas the Protestant missions draw their whole supplies from their mother countries the Catholics extract a good proportion of theirs from the soil on which they labour. It might be that some regulation could be applied to this branch of husbandry should it be anywhere found to offend the prejudices of the people.

Were the Protestant missions an organised body like the Romanists, the problem of a general reconciliation would lose some of its most intractable characters. For they could then speak and be spoken to, which is not possible under actual conditions. Each one of their thousand is as good as another, and, in his own eyes, perhaps better; and the societies themselves retain so much of the unregenerate man as to nourish a very human jealousy of each other. Signs are, however, beginning to be observed of both individuals and societies becoming alive to the serious evils of the schismatical spirit; the periodical conferences at Shanghai seem to be the heralds of a closer communion, and in Japan the necessities of the position have prompted a wider federation among sects and societies than has ever yet been attempted in China. The sense of disorganisation has indeed pressed so strongly on some of the more progressive missionaries that, throwing over the traditions of their fathers, they have declared openly for Episcopacy as the true and scriptural form of Church government. So effective a teacher is experience, when illuminated by common-sense and fortified by moral courage, that Mr. Gilbert Reid, born and bred Presbyterian, has been able to prove to his own satisfaction that Episcopacy is the very constitution which the missionary body in China requires. The need of a recognised head of the various Protestant missions has been often felt, and on one occasion at least Her Majesty's Government was obliged to attempt communication with them through the Bishop of Hongkong. It is of course a far cry from the tentative academical discussion of such advanced views to their actual adoption in practice; and it is at least premature to consider seriously the episcopalisation of the China missionaries, still more so their being ever marshalled under one Pope. But the immense waste of power, as well as the unregulated diversity of the doctrines taught, which is caused by the present system of promiscuous individualism, must continue to weigh upon the minds of great numbers of the missionaries. And as there are many earnest hearts and able heads in the camp, who knows but that, under the irresistible leading of events, they may make discoveries as to the permanent interest of Christ's Church in China (especially when in constant proximity to conflagration) which will make even the cripples among them take up their beds and walk?

Whatever may be the future order, however, the present state of things is equally intolerable to all the parties concerned, and is fraught with far-reaching disaster.

September, 1891.

APPENDIX I.

Rev. L. E. Louvet, of the Missions Etrangères, wrote in *Les Missions Catholiques*, 26th June, 1891 : *

"In this nineteenth century great efforts are being made for the conversion of China. From five the number of missionaries has increased to thirty—that of Christians has risen to more than half a million. Are we at last then to see the sunlight of Gospel truth shine on this great empire ? Alas! after ninety years of striving, the situation from a religious point of view appears to be more involved than ever.

"It is of no use to hide the fact: China obstinately rejects Christianity. The haughty men of letters are more rancorous than ever; every year incendiary placards call the people to the extermination of the foreign devils; and the day is approaching when this fine Church of China, that has cost so much trouble to the Catholic Apostolate, will be utterly destroyed, in the blood of her apostles and her children.

"Whence comes this obstinate determination to reject Christianity ? It is not religious fanaticism, for no people are so far gone as the Chinese in scepticism and indifference. One may be a disciple of Confucius or of Lao-tze, Mussulman or Buddhist, the Chinese Government does not regard it. It is only against the Christian religion it seeks to defend itself. It sees all Europe following on the heels of the Apostles of Christ, Europe with her ideas, her civilisation, and with *that* it will have absolutely

* This was, of course, written long before the outbreaks of 1891.

nothing to do, being, rightly or wrongly, satisfied with the ways of its fathers.

"The question, therefore, has much more of a political than a religious character, or rather it is almost entirely political. On the day when intelligent China shall be persuaded that it is possible to be Chinese and Christian at the same time—above all, on the day when she shall see a native ecclesiastic at the head of the Church in China, Christianity will obtain liberty in this great empire of 400 million souls, whose conversion will carry with it that of the Far East.

"The efforts of the missionaries should therefore be directed towards separating their cause entirely from all political interests. From this point of view I cannot for my own part but deplore the intervention of European governments. Nothing could in itself indeed be more legitimate, but at the same time nothing could be more dangerous or more likely to arouse the national pride and the hatred of the intellectual and learned classes. In truth, even from the special point of view of the safety of the missionaries, what have we gained by the provisions of the treaties? During the first forty years of the present century three missionaries only were put to death for the faith, after judicial sentence, viz., the Ven. Dufresse, Vicar-Apostolic of Sechuan, in 1814; the Ven. Clet and the Blessed Perboyre, Lazarists, in Hupei, in 1820 and 1840. Since the Treaties of 1844 and 1860 not a single death sentence has been judically pronounced, it is true, but more than twenty missionaries have fallen by the hands of assassins hired by the mandarins. These were: in 1856, the Ven. Chapdelaine; in 1862, the Ven. Néel; in 1865, 1869, 1873, MM. Mabileau, Rigaud, and Hue, in Sechuan; in 1874, M. Baptifau in Yunnan; in 1885, M. Terasse in Yunnan. Did the treaties prevent the horrible Tientsin massacre in June, 1870, the murder of our Consul, of all the French residents, of two

Lazarists, and nine Sisters of Charity? Nearly every year Christian communities are destroyed, churches sacked, missionaries killed or maimed, Christians put to death. And when France protests against such outrages she is answered by an insolent memorandum (1871) filled with calumnies against the missionaries and their works; and the chief of the embassy sent to Paris to excuse the massacres of Tientsin is the very man who directed them, and whose hands are still stained with the blood of our countrymen!

"Of course I give full credit to the zeal of our Consuls and Ministers. In almost every case they have given us hearty and loyal support, even those who, not possessing the joy of being Christians themselves, appeared unprepared by their antecedents to defend in China the religion they had persecuted at home. Nearly always sectarian hatred has been forgotten in national honour, and he who expelled the Jesuits from France proclaimed himself their friend and protector in Peking.

"It is not therefore the zeal of our diplomatic agents that I find wanting. I am only concerned to show their impotence.

"Rightly or wrongly, China will not have European civilisation which, in combination with Christianity, is to them simply the invasion of Europe.

"Let us then distinctly separate the religious from the political question.

"Needless to add that this is a strictly individual opinion, for I have no authority to speak for the missions, and I am well aware that among the missionaries opinion on this subject is divided. But being thoroughly convinced in my own mind I thought I might, without inconvenience, avail myself of the liberty granted by the Church to every one to publish and defend, in moderation, any honest conviction."

APPENDIX II.

MEMORIAL TO THE THRONE BY THE TSUNG-LI YAMÊN RESPECTING THE RECENT OUTRAGES ON THE YANGTZE, 26TH JULY, 1891.

The Prince and Ministers of the Tsung-li Yamôn reverently submit a Memorial to the Throne in which, with the view of ensuring the tranquility of the country and the prevention of future trouble, they humbly beg that His Majesty may be pleased to issue stringent instructions to the Viceroys and Governors of the various provinces directing them to take prompt measures for dealing with the missionary cases which have been occurring with such persistent frequency.

On learning, during the fourth moon of the present year, that the missionary establishments at Wuhu had been demolished, the Yamôn telegraphed at once to the Superintendent of Trade for the South asking him to send a gunboat to maintain order and afford protection, and desiring him to depute an officer to investigate the circumstances on the spot. Anonymous placards having been posted and false rumours circulated simultaneously at Anch'ingfu, Shanghai, and other places, the Superintendent was likewise requested to direct all his subordinates to redouble their precautions. Later on the Southern Superintendent of Trade and the Governor of Anhui reported by telegraph that the Wuhu affair had its origin in false rumours that were spread about female missionary doctors kidnapping young children. The popular suspicion could not be allayed until a crowd collected and a riot took place which resulted in the missionary premises being burnt down by the mob. Two of the ringleaders were subsequently arrested and summarily decapitated by way of warning. The district had resumed its normal peaceful condition. After a very short interval, however, the burning of the missionary establishment at Tanyang took place, and this was followed by the destruction of similar premises at Wusüeh, in Hupeh, the particulars of which have not yet been fully ascertained, although it is reported that two foreigners were murdered. In addition to the above there have been serious riots at Nanking and Kiukiang, but fortunately the Imperial troops had taken effectual precautions and immediately suppressed the disturbance.

All this continual trouble has had a very disquieting effect amongst both Chinese and foreigners. In investigating the cause of the present state of things, it will be found that it arises from the great number of disbanded soldiers and of the criminal classes connected with secret societies who are to be found everywhere in the provinces bordering upon the Yangtze. The movement is one with which the well-disposed portion of the population has nothing to do, and its object is to influence the minds of the people by the dissemination of placards and to make use of the opportunity to create certain trouble.

The religion of the West has for its object the inculcation of virtue, and in Western countries it is everywhere practised. Its origin dates a long time past, and on the establishment of commercial intercourse between China and Foreign Powers, a clause was inserted in the Treaties to the effect that "persons professing or teaching the Christian religion should enjoy full protection of their persons and property and be allowed free exercise of their religion." The hospitals and orphanages maintained by the missionaries all evince a spirit of benevolent enterprise. Of late years when distress has befallen any portion of the Empire, missionaries and others have never failed to come forward to assist the sufferers by subscribing money and distributing relief. For their cheerful readiness to do good and the pleasure they take in works of charity they assuredly deserve high commendation. Even granting that amongst the converts there are bad as well as good people, still they are all equally Chinese subjects, amenable to the jurisdiction of their own authorities, and the missionary cannot claim the right of interfering in any disputes or lawsuits that may arise. There is no reason, therefore, why the people and the converts should not live together in peace and harmony. Yet mischief-makers are continually fabricating baseless stories which they industriously propagate until the suspicions of the people are aroused, and then lawless villains seize the opportunity to create trouble with a view to obtaining plunder. If immediate steps are not taken to prevent outbreaks of this kind, both the Chinese and the foreign mercantile community will, it is to be feared, have no assurance of safety in the future, and the very important interests involved cannot fail to be seriously prejudiced.

The Yamên would therefore pray that the Manchu General-in-Chief, the Viceroy, and Governors of all the provinces may be directed by Imperial edict to issue proclamations clearly expounding to the people that they must on no account lend a ready ear to such false reports and wantonly cause trouble. People who issue anonymous placards and invent stories to inflame the feelings of the people should, it is submitted, be at once arrested and severely punished. It is the duty of the local authorities to afford protection at all times to the persons and property of foreign merchants and foreign missionaries, and no relaxation in this respect should be permitted. Should the precautionary measures be lacking in stringency or the protection afforded prove inadequate to avert disturbance, the local authorities should be denounced in accordance with the facts of the case.

… With regard to the various riots which form the subject of this memorial, and excluding the Wuhu case, the ringleaders in which have already suffered the full penalty of the law, it is essential that the Viceroys of the Two Kiang and of Hu Kuang, and the Governors of Kiangsu, Anhui, and Hupeh should receive prompt instructions to effect the arrest of the principal criminals, and have them severely punished as a warning for the future. The Manchu Generals-in-Chief, Viceroys, and Governors should be directed to take steps for settling all outstanding cases without delay, and should not allow their subordinates to shrink from the difficulty of the task and interpose delays.

The Yamên reverently submit this memorial to the Sacred Glance and humbly solicit His Majesty's commands respecting the suggestions they have ventured to offer.

APPENDIX III.

How an Anti-Christian Riot is Organised.

(Described by a Chinese Scholar.)

[Extract from an article in *North China Daily News*, September 16th, signed " F."]

In connection with this testimony of a foreigner to the origin of an anti-missionary riot, I wish now to call special attention to the account of a similar riot, or rather of a very much worse one, given in the Chinese Blue Books by a Chinaman from a Chinese standpoint. The writer himself was behind the scenes and tells us just how everything was managed, who were the responsible persons and what part each of them played in the game. This account will be found in the chapter on " The expulsion of Christianity from Kiangsi and Hunan," mentioned in my last paper. It appears to be extracted from the 'Chinese and Foreign Record.' That book is, I believe, published anonymously, but the author speaks of himself as an actor in some of the scenes he relates, and from what he says of the part he played, he must have been some sort of responsible official in Kiangsi.

He tells us that in 1862 a French priest having asked for a passport to enable him to travel, went to Hunan. The Roman Catholics of Changsha and Hsiangtan hearing that he was coming, were delighted, but the gentry when they heard of it were disgusted. They issued placards and held a consultation in regard to expelling the Roman Catholics. [The placards stated that] if anyone let houses to the priests the houses were to be burnt; if anyone entered the sect, his name was to be struck off the register of his clan and his children were to be forbidden for ever to enter the examinations. All this was to be done principally because these priests use the name of preaching to cover their designs of immorality and to establish orphanages for disgraceful purposes, which things the gentry graphically and fully described, sending the description on to Kiangsi. When Lo Ngan-t'ang, a foreign priest, came with his passport to the provincial capital of Nanchang, in Kiangsi, he was detained, and proceeded no further. The examinations were about to be held, and the leading gentry of Nanchang met together in full force in the Yu-chang college. There were present Hia T'ing-kü, an official in the Hanlin Yuan who was on furlough, Liu Yü-sin, an ex-provincial judge of the province of Kansu, and others. They took the Hunan placard and, raising a subscription, got a printer within 24 hours to print off some tens of thousands of copies, and with them they covered all the walls in the principal thoroughfares of the city, both within and without. When the Frenchman heard of it he went to see the mandarins. It happened to be immediately after the accession of the Emperor T'ung Chi [and some changes were taking place amongst the high officials]. The new Governor Shên Pao-chêng had not yet arrived. The Treasurer of the province, Li Pu-t'ang, who had just been promoted to this office and who had charge of the Governor's seals, refused to see the Frenchman, on the ground that the Governor himself would arrive in five days. When Shên Pao-chêng came the priest went to him with his complaint, but he would not see him. Then he tried to pay the Governor a visit of ceremony, but with no better success, whereat he was disappointed. It being the time of the examinations the Literary Chancellor was also in Nanchang. On the 17th day of the second month I [i.e. the writer of this narrative] was examining the essays of the candidates in the prefect's *yamên* when about midday the prefect Wang Hia-hien and a servant of the district Magistrate came in hastily to tell me that placards had been posted up everywhere saying that next day at noon the Roman Catholic church would be wrecked, and they said if the people were stirred up there would be a riot which would cause inconvenience not only to the responsible local mandarins, but to the minor officials also. I said " What is to be done?" They both replied, " Hia Ting-kû the Hanlin can give what orders he likes in the college, and although he may not have planned (the riot) he can stop it." I replied " He has been drinking all day and now his door is shut and he will not see visitors, but my son knows a good many of his servants, and I will tell him to go and see how things are." So I went back to my lodging and told my son to go at once on horseback to the place, but just as he was starting a messenger came from the French priest Lo, and another named Fang, saying that the orphanage had been looted. His master, he said, was safe and had gone away through the Fucheu gate of the city, but the girls from the orphanage were missing, and it looked as if the trouble might extend to the church outside the city, and he wished to know if we would protect him. I at once went with the district magistrate Chang to the *yamên* of the prefect where there were two other district magistrates. We then went together to the Kwai-tsz-hang (the street in Nanchang where the church and orphanage of the mission were situated). In addition to destroying the orphanage the mob had also torn down some tens of houses in which the converts lived. It was already getting dark and the city gate had been shut, so we went back to inform the Governor of what had happened. When he heard it he sighed and said, "These foreigners have troubled me for a long time, and now quite unexpectedly our people have taken the matter in hand and paid them out. Although we shall be blamed for mismanaging things, I will take the responsibility upon myself. Don't talk of searching for the offenders and apprehending them. I will report the facts (to Peking) and ask that I may be severely dealt with, and no enquiries will be made about the doings of the local mandarins and of their assistants." On the 18th of the month, i.e. next day, the old Roman Catholic church outside the city was destroyed, and a boat in which the missionaries were, was destroyed also—both by night. The French priests Lo and Fang got away in different directions. The former went to Fucheu and found shelter on the road at the house of a convert named Ch'ên. . . . The people sought for him and could not find him, but they destroyed several houses belonging to the Ch'ên family.

The sequel to this disgraceful story, itself even yet more disgraceful, must be told in connection with the machinations of the *literati* to discredit the orphanage work of the missionaries and to cause even the very name of orphanage to excite the fury of the people, as a red rag flourished about before the eyes of a bull is said to infuriate to madness a beast that, if left alone, would be perfectly harmless. By the foregoing passage, translated from the Blue Books Supplement, two things are made perfectly clear: firstly, that both in Hunan and also in Kiangsi, it was not the common people, but the "educated" classes who first manifested the anti-foreign feeling and desired to expel the foreigner with violence. What we call "the common people" the Chinese rulers always call "the stupid people." Now these "stupid people" if left alone are generally stupid enough to leave the foreigner alone, but when once their superiors take them in hand and see how much they can teach them in a short time about foreign men and foreign things, there seems to be no limit to their powers of receptivity. They can believe anything, however absurd and however vile, and when worked up to a white heat by means of placards and handbills, and assured of plunder, with immunity from all danger of being punished for stealing, they are ready for anything. Secondly, it is clear that the most guilty persons in the transactions connected with the expulsion of Christians from Kiangsi in 1862, were not even the irresponsible "gentry," but the officials themselves.

APPENDIX IV.

Abstract of Mission Statistics in China Proper:

Catholics:	530 Foreign Missionaries.
"	525,000 Native Christians.
Protestants:	589 Men.
"	391 Wives.
"	316 Single Women.
	1,296 Foreign Missionaries.
	37,287 Native Christians.

CATHOLIC MISSIONS AND STATISTICS.

The following table shows the names and nationalities of Catholic missions in China and its dependencies, the number of native Christians and foreign missionaries. From this table, compiled from a work published at Rome by the Congregation de Propaganda Fide in 1887, it will be seen that of the eighteen provinces of China, Mongolia, Manchuria, Tibet, and Corea, thirteen are in the hands of French missions, four in those of Italians, two in those of Belgians, one in those of a Spanish mission, while one province, Hunan, is divided between an Italian and a Spanish mission, and one, Shantung, between an Italian and a German one.

The Catholic missions working in China are: Spanish Dominicans and Austin Friars (Augustiniani); Italian Franciscans (Franciscales and Franciscales Reformati) and the Foreign Missions at Milan; German, from the College at Steyl; Belgian, the Congregation Immaculati Cordis Beatæ Virginis Mariæ at Scheutveld; French, the

Jesuits, the Lazarists (Congregation Missionis), the Foreign Missions of Paris (Seminaire des Missions Etrangères).

According to the nationality of the missions there would be 82 Italian, 28 Spanish, 14 German, 29 Belgian, and 400 French missionaries, but it is well known that between these latter there are a good many priests belonging to other nationalities than the French one.

Province or Locality.	Mission.	Nationality.	No. of Native Christians, Catechumens excepted.	No. of Foreign Missionaries.
Amoy (Formosa)	Dominicans	Spanish	3,685	9
Shansi	Franciscans	Italian	14,980	7
Shantung {North	„	„	16,016	12
{South	College at Steyl	German	823	14
Shensi	Franciscans	Italian	21,300	15
Fukien	Dominicans	Spanish	32,400	15
Honan {North	Foreign Missions of Milan	Italian	1,235	3
{South	„ „	„	5,000	6
Hong-kong	„ „	„	6,800	7
Hunan {North	Austin Friars	Spanish	100	4
{South	Franciscans	Italian	5,000	4
Hupei {North-west	„	„	6,192	8
{East	„	„	13,005	14
{South-west	„	„	4,109	6
Kansu	Congregation Imm. Cordis B. M. V. of Scheutveld	Belgian	1,500	5
Kiangnan	Jesuits	French	103,815	83
Kiangsi {North	Lazarists	„	3,211	5
{East	„	„	10,861	10
{South	„	„	3,753	3
Kuangsi	Foreign Missions of Paris	„	1,013	11
Kuangtung	„ „	„	28,668	39
Kueichow	„ „	„	16,892	26
Scchuan {North-east	„ „	„	38,800	24
{East	„ „	„	26,079	31
{South	„ „	„	18,000	23
Chekiang	Lazarists	„	7,480	9
Chihli {North	„	„	32,761	19
{South-east	Jesuits	„	34,530	37
{South-west	Lazarists	„	26,244	10
Yünnan	Foreign Missions of Paris	„	11,207	12
Manchuria	„ „	„	12,530	26
Mongolia {East	Congregation Imm. Cordis B. M. V. of Scheutveld	Belgian	5,500	7
{Middle	„ „	„	9,000	14
{South-west	„ „	„	3,000	3
Tibet	Foreign Missions of Paris	French	991	13
Corea	„ „	„	13,642	10
			539,215	553

www.ingramcontent.com/pod-product-compliance
Lightning Source LLC
Chambersburg PA
CBHW031355160426
43196CB00007B/825